JOACHIM S[

Ice Memory
Selected Poems

Translated by
Richard Dove
Robert Gray
Michael Hamburger
Michael Hulse
Christopher Middleton
Sibylle Schlesier
Andrew Shields
Nathaniel Tarn
Rosmarie Waldrop

Edited by
Richard Dove

With an afterword by
Christopher Middleton

CARCANET

First published in Great Britain in 2006 by
Carcanet Press Limited
Alliance House
Cross Street
Manchester M2 7AQ

All poems by Joachim Sartorius reprinted by kind permission of the
publishers.

Poems from *Sage ich zu wem* by Joachim Sartorius © 1988 by Verlag
Kiepenheuer & Witsch, Köln.
Poems from *Der Tisch wird kalt* by Joachim Sartorius © 1992 by Verlag
Kiepenheuer & Witsch, Köln.
Poems from *Keiner gefriert anders* by Joachim Sartorius © 1996 by Verlag
Kiepenheuer & Witsch, Köln.
Poems from *Ich habe die Nacht* by Joachim Sartorius © 2003 DuMont
Literatur und Kunst Verlag, Köln.

English translations © individual translators 2006
Selection © Richard Dove 2006
Afterword © Christopher Middleton 2006

A CIP catalogue record for this book is available from the British Library
ISBN 1 85754 832 9
978 1 85754 832 7

The publisher acknowledges financial assistance from
Arts Council England

Typeset by XL Publishing Services, Tiverton
Printed and bound in England by SRP Ltd, Exeter

Ice Memory

JOACHIM SARTORIUS was born in 1946 in Fürth / Franconia and grew up in Tunis. He studied law and political science in Munich, London and Paris, and served as a diplomat in New York, Istanbul, Prague and Nicosia until 1986. After holding various positions in the field of international cultural policy, he acted as head of the Goethe Institute worldwide. Since 2001 he has been Director General of the Berlin Festivals. He has received fellowships from the Rockefeller Foundation and the Budapest Collegium and was elected a fellow of the German Academy for Language and Literature in 2002. Joachim Sartorius holds a professorship at the University of Arts in Berlin, where he lives.

His wide-ranging publishing projects include translations of the collected works of Malcolm Lowry and William Carlos Williams, as well as of works by John Ashbery, Wallace Stevens and Allen Curnow, among many others; book collaborations with the artists James Lee Byars, Nan Goldin and Max Neumann; and the highly regarded international poetry anthology *Atlas der neuen Poesie* (1995). His own poetry has been collected in five volumes, and is now also available in Arabic, Dutch, French, Greek, Hungarian, Romanian and Spanish editions. Joachim Sartorius was recently awarded the Paul Scheerbart Prize for his translations of contemporary American poetry.

Contents

from *Sage ich zu wem* / *To someone I say* (1988)

from *Der Tisch wird kalt* / *The table grows cold* (1992)

from Keiner gefriert anders / No one freezes differently (1996)

from *Ich habe die Nacht / Mine is the night* (2003)

Contents   vii

Acknowledgements

Some of these translations, or earlier versions of them, were published in the following magazines and anthologies: *Conjunctions* 23: *New World Writing* (1994); *Mouth to Mouth: Contemporary German Poetry in Translation*, ed. Thomas Wohlfahrt and Tobias Lehmkuhl (Giramondo Publishing Company, Artarmon NSW, Australia, 2004); *Poetry* November 1998 (Chicago); *PN Review* 158 (2004) (Christopher Middleton); *PN Review* 159 (2004) (Robert Gray).

The title poem was inspired by an essay of Elizabeth Kolbert's in the *New Yorker* (2002).

Thanks are also due to the team of translators which has resourcefully teased out the various strands of this many-sided writer, important not least for having reconciled the short ('hermetic') with the long ('dialectical') poem, but essential for having demonstrated in his 'broken modern West-Eastern Divan' how bridges can be built in the shadow of 9/11.

Richard Dove
2006

from
Sage ich zu wem
To someone I say
(1988)

Umarmung, con affeto

die Hände wie Kreisel, fühlen deine
bemalten Zehen, Brüste, Gewebespannungen
zwischen glänzenden Ameisen, fühlen:
rosa an der Spitze die Nacht, Ummantelung –
die Flöte tanzt wie eine Feder, Formentera!
auf dem Metronom, dir meine
Zunge in der Mandelkurve deiner
innersten Lippe, ja ich läge ja sehnlichst
läge ich in dir in deines Körpers Laken-Nacht
ein Jagen die Hügel hinauf ein Hineinsteigen
ins Hochgrab durch das – reglos – ein Wasserfall
fällt tief in den umpelzten Kragenmund tiefe
Ausgrabungen unter den Brüsten Schürfungen
zwei Erhebungen aus Wasser Milch schäumt das Tal
jetzt fühlst du die heißen Kiesel jetzt
in deinen tiefen Mund zum Schlunde zielen
Moos Gold den Schlamm saugst du hinein
und dunkel sperrt und öffnet sich die Gracht

from *Sage ich zu wem*

Embrace, con affeto

these hands, like spinning-tops, feel your
painted toes, breasts, tissue rippling
between gleaming ants, feel
pink at its tip the enveloping night –
the flute is dancing like a feather, Formentera!
on the metronome, for you
my tongue in the almond curve of your
innermost lip, o yes how ardently I'd be lying
if lying in you in your body's linen-night
racing up the hills climbing into
that grave, high grave, through which – motionless – a waterfall's
pouring deep into that fur-protected collar-mouth deep
excavations beneath the breasts abrasions
two elevations of water milk is the valley foaming
now you feel the hot pebbles now
homing in on your deep mouth to the deep south
moss gold you suck in the slush
and darkly the gracht closes, opens

Richard Dove

Umarmung erinnert

Deinen Atem fühlen, vom Hals aus:
fühlen, wie er um meinen Leib geht,
und in dir drängen und deine Augen
schlucken wollt ich: wortkrank, und
schlittrig ist das Erinnern. Und die Lippe,
die meiner Lippe jetzt begegnet, sie ist
die andere Hälfte meines Munds. Ich
wurde schön in deinem Körper, ohne
Schmerz wurd ich, und Ungenutztes
tauchte, herauf schoß es in Fächern,
schoßwärts aufgeschlagen, und Armespiel.

Im Bild ist sie, klein und nackt,
aufgenommen vor der Tür des Hauses
vom Freund oder Vater, mit verlegenen
Brüsten, furchtsamem Dreieck, sie kann mich
nicht hören noch sehen. Ich, ich entsinne
mich genau des braunen Grases, das zwischen
den Stufen wuchs, unserer Sprache auch,
Blaues ließ sie um uns wie Löcher
in den Ozeanen. Nein, in eine
neue Geschichte zu tauchen sei nicht schwer.
Und höre ihr Atmen durch die Sehnacht gehen

from *Sage ich zu wem*

Remembered embrace

To feel your breath, from down at your neck:
to feel it flowing around my body;
I longed to throng inside you and swallow
your eyes: remembrance is word-
sick and slippery. And the lip
now meeting my lip
is the other half of my mouth. Inside
your body I became comely,
pain-free and unused things
dived down, shot up fanwise,
opened wombwards, amid the interplay of arms.

She's there, small and naked, in the picture
taken in front of the door of the house
by her boyfriend or father, with embarrassed
breasts, a fearful triangle; she can't
either hear or see me; I,
I exactly recall the brown grass growing
between the steps, recall our words:
they left blue space around us like holes
in the oceans. No, to dive
into a new story is not all that hard, or so it is said.
And I hear her breathing flowing through the night of seeing

Richard Dove

Umarmung der Vögel

Wie ging die Sage: die Falkinnen
(es gab keinen Falken weit und breit)
hielten mitten im Flug plötzlich inne,
reglos schwebten sie da und öffneten
ihren Schoß und empfingen vom Wind
ihren Samen und Frucht. Die eine hat sich
an meine Wiege gesetzt, sagte Leonardo,
und mit ihrem Schwanz mir den Mund
geöffnet und das Gefieder heftig darin
bewegt. Uccello wollte die Lichtreflexe
auf Pferderücken ergründen, wie nach ihm
auf Frauenarmen Bonnard; seither, sagte Leonardo,
forsche ich den Flug der Vögel, sein Geheimnis.

‚Den Flug der Vögel in der Luft und die Spur
des Mannes in der jungen Frau…' an meiner
Wiege sitzst du, den Traum des langen
Speers im Doppelauge. Wir schauen uns
an, ich denke mich an deine Fieder-
schläfe, bevor die Hand noch sie
umkrallt. Gefaltet die weißen Flügel
über des anderen Rücken, Iris in Iris:
So liegen wir luftauf und schreien. Mein Speer,
dein Federzeug schnabelweis in Mund und Mund
schweben wir, reglos: ein Leichtwerden von
mir zu dir, ohne Qual, fernlos, wie Gleiten
auf Lichtkufen, und wieder sein Geheimnis neu.

from *Sage ich zu wem*

Embrace of the birds

This is the legend: the falconesses
(no falcons were found then far and wide)
stopped suddenly in mid-flight,
hung motionless and opened
their wombs and received from the wind
the seed and fruit. One of them, said Leonardo,
alighted on my cradle
and with its tail-feathers opened my mouth
and violently moved that appendage
in there. Uccello was out to get to the bottom
of light-refractions on horses' backs, and after him
Bonnard on women's arms. Since then, said Leonardo,
I've been studying bird-flight, its mystery.

'The flight of the birds in the air and the trace
of the man in the young woman...' On my
cradle you are sitting, the dream of the long
spear in our over-lapping gaze. We look at each
other, I think myself into your feathery
brow, back before the hand closed
its claws around it. The white wings are folded
above the other's back; iris to iris
we lie upon the air and shriek. My spear,
your feathers beakwise, in mouth and mouth,
we float unmoving: a light expands from
me to you, without torment, or distance, like gliding
on light-runners; and again its mystery is new.

Robert Gray

Memento Mori

Deine Haut aus schwärenden Blättern
die Wolken über dem Dach

Du steigst immer wieder aus meinem Scheitern auf
größer als ein Tempel kälter als der Wind
der das Gedächtnis leerfegt und
befriedet. Seligsprechung. Betörungen: Glaub mir
ich wollte den Schrecken nicht um unsere Nacken
schlingen
          späte Vögel sende ich zu den Bäumen
die du jetzt auf dem Rücken trägst
                              die Erde
unter meinem Farngesicht bist du, im Wider-
hell das Innere dunkel herstellmöglich, bist
diese Erde du? Wie weit trägt Trauerarbeit,
da du von mir in mir nun bist? Wiederhole:
Niemand sieht dich. Nicht die Wolken, nicht
die Blätter. Nicht ich, und sende Vögel aus

verzweifelt: der Raum von meiner Stirn
zu deiner Maske soll nicht zu messen sein.

Memento mori

Your skin made of festering leaves
the clouds above the roof

Again and again you climb up out of my failure
larger than a temple colder than the wind
which sweeps the memory empty,
brings peace. Beatification. Enthrallments: believe me
I didn't want to wrap terror round
our necks
                late birds I send to the trees
which you're now carrying on your back
                              the earth
beneath my bracken-face is you, its inner
reaches dark against the glare, restorable, is
this earth you? How far does the work of mourning take us,
since you are now part of me, in me? Repeat:
no one sees you. The clouds don't, the
leaves don't. I don't either, and send out birds

it's told that the space from my forehead
to your mask cannot be measured.

Richard Dove

Das liebste Spiel

Du faltest mich ein
ungebärdig steif
und verstehst mich nicht.

Schön nur zu fallen

blind durch Himmel
und Hölle zu hüpfen:
Bin ich? Bin ich? Bin ich?

(denn hier wie vor dem Tod
strengt sich der Feigste an)

A favourite game

You fold me into you –
stiff, unruly –
and don't understand me.

How good just to fall

to blindly leap through
heaven and hell:
Am I? Am I? Am I?

(for here as before death
even the greatest faintheart tries hard)

Richard Dove

Liebe und Arbeit

Du sagst das Ende der Liebe voraus
Hör auf Liebe ist ein Wort
wie Geduld oder Verschwendung
Es arbeitet es ist da
damit wir uns darauf einlassen
wie auf ein Ultramarin zwischen Felsblöcken
Es ist eine Farbe ein Weg eine Arbeit
des Zugehens es ist eine Hoffnung
die wir nähren müssen
Erst wenn die Liebe keinen Wein
mehr erhält
können wir das Wort streichen

Nimm ein Wort wie Schneebruch So
stürzen die Worte unter dem Nirgends
nieder wenn wir sie nicht nutzen
sie wandern von Lippe zu Lippe
sie stürzen in die schwarze Erde
wenn dem Ast das Wort nicht
ins Nadeln fällt
Nicht jeder hat die Gabe
der Worte Aber wenn wir Liebe haben
und in uns arbeiten dann stehen wir
fest zwischen den Millionen von Bäumen
Ferne wird eine Kategorie der Nähe

und wir können leben

from *Sage ich zu wem*

Love and work

You foretell the end of love
Quit it Love is a word
like patience or like waste
It works it is here
for us to respond to as to a
flash of ultra-marine between some rocks
It is a colour a path a travail
of coming closer it is a hope
we have to nourish
Only when love gets
no wine any more
can we delete the word

Take a word like snowbreak That's
how words plummet down beneath
Nowhere when we do not use them
they raptly pass from lip to lip
they plummet down into the black earth
when the word does not interrupt
the branch's needle-shedding
Not everyone has the gift
of words But if we have love
and do not spare ourselves then we stand
firm between the millions of trees
Distance becomes a category of closeness

and we can live

Richard Dove

Das Schweigen von Zypern

I

‚Nichts hier außer ein Chaos von Felsen, der Fluß
und das Meer. Die Hitze ist sehr stark. Man muß
in der Wüste am Rand des Meeres schlafen. Ich
schreibe euch das in der Wüste und weiß nicht,
wann ich es aufgeben kann.'

auf Schienen, verworren, verstummt
nach dem Sägenschnitt durch die Lebenszeit,
Lebensreise, der Rücken noch so gepanzert.

‚Ich bin jetzt Aufseher im Palast, den man
für den Generalgouverneur auf dem Troodos
(2.100 m) baut. Es ist nichts auf dem Berg
außer Tannen und Farn. Schickt mir schnellstens
das Handbuch der forst- und landwirtschaftlichen
Sägereien, 3 Francs, mit 128 Abbildungen.'

Die Geschichte ist wie eine Eisenbahn,
durchsichtig wie Spielzeug,
zwischen Charleville und Harrar.

‚Wenn ich ein paar hundert Francs zusammen
habe, gehe ich nach Sansibar,
wo es, wie man sagt, zu tun gibt.'

Die Menschen hier sind Verwünschungen.
Auch wenn es für sie spricht, daß sie
schlafen können, wenn vom See an ihrer Tür
das Salz hochkriecht, von Tränen geweint,
eimerweise.

‚Es wird draus, was draus wird.'

(Sonntag, 23.5.1880, Troodos-Berg)

from *Sage ich zu wem*

The Cyprus silence

I

'Nothing here but a jumble of rocks, the river
and the sea. The heat is overwhelming. One has to
sleep in the desert on the sea's edge. I'm
writing you this in the desert and don't know
when I can get it into the post.'

on rails, all tangled, silenced
after a lifetime sawn through,
life's journey, however armoured my back.

'I'm foreman now at the palace being built
for the Governor-General on the Troodos
(2100 metres high). There's nothing on the mountain
but fir trees and ferns. Send me express
the handbook of forest and agricultural
sawmills, 3 francs, with 128 plates.'

History is like a railway,
transparent as a toy,
between Charleville and Harrar.

'When I've put together a few
hundred francs I shall go to Zanzibar
where, they say, there's something doing.'

The people here are curses.
Even if it speaks for them that they
can sleep when from the lake at their door
salt creeps up, wept by tears,
by the bucketful.

'What will come of it is what comes of it.'

(Sunday, 23.5.1880, Mount Troodos)

II

‚Vitalie sagte vor ihrem Tod, mein Kopf sei
geschrumpft. Das war vor Batavia, vor Zypern,
ich hatte mit dem Schreiben längst aufgehört.
Die Haut ist zu groß. In zärtlichen Momenten
nannte sie mich: mein Leguan.'

Alles verwandelt sich. Unsere Schrift,
unser Fleisch, auch die Liebe. Daraus,
und daß wir nie heimisch werden,
entsteht das Gedicht. (Sinnlos selbst das,
verschwindet an einer Mauer.)

‚Und ich weiß jetzt nichts mehr.
Nichts, nichts, nichts. Nur
wenig zu verbinden gelingt noch:
den Körper zum Leben, das wartet.
Ich schaue auf die Zeit, ich kaue
die Zeit. Ich bin alt (nicht an Jahren).
Ich bin gelangweilt. Ich taste
nach dem Gold in meinem Gürtel,
meine Sicherheit. Der Palast jedenfalls
ist etwas Stabiles. Und ich sage euch,
Wahrheit ist ein Wunder.'

Unser Körper ist der Pilze Beute.
Darüber glüht die Sonne
auf dem Farn nach,
darüber roter Staub,
darüber, noch einmal: nichts.

(Samstag 11.10.1986, Larnaka)

from *Sage ich zu wem*

II

'Vitalie said before her death that my head
had shrunk. That was before Batavia, before Cyprus,
I'd long ceased to scribble.
There's too much skin. At tender moments
she called me "my iguana".'

Everything changes. Our handwriting,
our flesh, love too. From this,
and that we never feel at home,
poetry springs. (This, too, is meaningless,
it vanishes from a wall.)

'And now I know nothing any more.
Nothing. Nothing. Nothing. To connect
a little is all I can do:
the body to life that's a waiting.
I count on time, I chew on
time. I'm old (not in years).
I'm bored. I fumble
at the gold in my belt,
my security. The palace at least
is something stable. And I tell you,
truth is a miracle.'

Our bodies are food for fungus.
Above these an afterglow
of the sun on fern,
above that, red dust,
above that again: nothing.

(Saturday, 11.10.1986, Larnaka)

Michael Hamburger

Der Kultstein von Kouklia

Es ist ein Meteorit.
Ein Steinbrocken, dessen Feuer
beim Aufprall erlosch. Die dünne
gläserne Schmelzrinde erinnert
an dieses Zusammentreffen
von Himmel und Erde, sie
zieht die Suchenden an.

Er ist unansehnlich, graugrün
statt schwarz, die Kegelform
nicht regelmäßig, ein Idol,
das keinen Reim gibt
auf die schöngestaltige
Schaumgeborene. Es wird
das Geheimnis der Wallfahrt
sein.

Die hohen, sich selbst tragenden
Säulen, gekrönt vom Doppelhorn,
sind auf Münzen zu sehen.
Das reine Feuer, das zum Himmel
stieg, müssen wir uns denken.
Wir wandern um den Glassturz.
Vor dem Museum donnern Lastwagen,
beladen mit antikem Marmor,
über die Straßen der Erinnerung.
Der Stein kann nicht berührt,
nicht geküßt werden.

from *Sage ich zu wem*

The cultic stone of Kouklia

It's a meteorite –
lump of stone whose fire
went out on impact. The thin
and glassy fusion crust reminds
of this meeting
of heaven and earth: it
draws onlookers to it.

This boulder's unsightly, grey-green
not black, its conical shape
not regular, an idol
that fails to chime with,
rhyme with, the fair-limbed
foam-born goddess. This
will be the pilgrimage's
secret.

The tall self-supporting
pillars, crowned with twin horns,
are to be seen on coins.
The pure fire which ascended
to heaven we have to imagine.
We shuffle aimlessly round the glass-dome.
Outside the museum, trucks thunder,
loaded with ancient marble,
down the roads of memory.
The stone cannot be touched,
be kissed.

Richard Dove

Die Nekropole von Nizza

Das Krematorium der Stadt Nizza,
eingezäunt, 10 km aufwärts am Var,
zwischen Kleinindustrie und Mangoldfeldern,
gebaut in ein felsiges Amphitheater
wie ein moderner Tempel für Hatschepsut,
Arabesken aus Leichtbeton, weiß, bombastisch,
sinnlose Versatzstücke der Callablüte
und des Mohnstengels, unwirklich, lumpig
und bedrängt, umzäunt, baumlos:
Platz für 60.000 Urnen.
Der Wind orgelt über den Parkplatz,
als zerstöhne sich die Asche noch.
Zwei Wärter, Nordafrikaner,
Gesichter, die auf Prügel warten,
hissen Butanflaschen
auf eine Lorre, die ins Innere fährt
im Glanz der Stabtaschenlampen.

The necropolis of Nice

The crematorium for the city of Nice
is fenced in, ten kilometres up the Var,
between small industries and mangold fields:
an amphitheatre built in a quarry,
like a modern temple for Queen Hatchepsut.
Arabesques ornament lightweight concrete
with white bombast: set pieces of the canna bloom
and of poppy stalks. Ragged
and plagued, sunken and treeless,
a place of sixty thousand urns.
The wind organs over the car park, as if ash still groans.
Two guards, north African,
faces that wait for a beating,
hoist bottles of butane
onto a trolley, and these are pushed toward the interior
in a gleam of flashlights.

Robert Gray

100 Bleecker Street

Du wachst
mit den reinsten und besten Absichten auf,
es ist Abend, du holst dir die Dächer
der Wolkenkratzer heran: Das Leben
ist dort. Antennen hoch wie Häuser,
Lichtsignale, der Tanz der Radare, Metalle
leicht wie Luft. Ein schöner Betrieb. Im
Fernglas kommen drei Helikopter heran, als
bauten sie gläubig auf die fernen Dächer.
Jetzt kämpfen die Stuntmänner gegen Hornissen,
jetzt sterben unten die Leute im Film
in den leeren erleuchteten Zimmern.
Ein nackter Arm. Du kannst nicht mehr
als die Achsel erkennen, den Ellenbogen,
davor das Fensterkreuz, das große Blatt
einer Pflanze. Ist es ein Arm? Er müßte
sich bewegen. Doch dein Herz ist
warm wie von einem guten Traum,
du hängst das Telefon aus und gehst
in deine Straßen, wo die Autos weiß sind
wie Kühlschränke, wie deine lautere Absicht,
wie dein Auge im schwarzen Aug des Glases.
Du knipst das Licht an. Einer sieht dich aus.

from *Sage ich zu wem*

100 Bleecker Street

You wake
up with the purest, with the best intentions,
it's evening, you home in on the roofs
of the skyscrapers: that's where
life hangs out. Antennae as tall as houses,
light signals, the dance of the radar, metals
as light as air. Smart bustle. Three choppers
swim into your ken, as though they were
piously putting their trust in the distant roofs.
Now the stuntmen are fighting with hornets,
now the guys in the film down there
are dying in the empty, illuminated rooms.
A naked arm. You can't make out
more than the armpit, the elbow;
in front there's a window-cross, the voluminous leaf
of a plant. Well, is it an arm? It ought
to be moving. However, your heart is
warm as though warmed by a happy dream;
you pull the phone out of the wall, go out
into your streets where the cars are white
as fridges, as your unalloyed intention,
as your eye in the glass's black eye.
You switch the light on. Somebody's stare takes you out.

Richard Dove

Am Arno bei Arezzo

Im Abstieg des Augs,
soweit es abblickt im grauen Geäst,
Fetzen von Plastiktüten, blauen,
grauen: tausende,
an schwarze Zweige geheftet
wie Gebetsfedern,
die Weiden mit Stoffstreifen
verknotete Talisbäume,

und zwischen
Girlanden, dem ganzen Zerriß
im dunklen Bett
der nicht erwärmende Fluß.
Fließt mit Tüten, Federn, Fetzen,
Kanistern starr
nach Florenz.

Das ist das Spiel: Zukunft
unter Vergangenes zu spülen,
oder das Vergangene so in die Zukunft
zu reißen, daß dort
die Toten auf uns warten,

freundlich, bewimpelt, nah.

from *Sage ich zu wem*

By the Arno near Arezzo

In the downward path of your eye,
as far down as it can see amid the grey of the branchwork,
shreds of plastic bags, blue,
grey: thousands
like prayer feathers
fixed to black boughs;
the willows are talistrees
knotted together with strips of fabric;

and, in between
festoons, that riot of laceration
in the dark bed:
the river incapable of warming.
It rigidly flows
with its bags, feathers, shreds,
cans down to Florence.

The name of the game: to wrench the future
into things past
or to wrest the past in such a manner
into the future that there
the dead are awaiting us,

affable, wimpled, a touch away.

Richard Dove

Porträt des Künstlers als alter Mann

*Überdies zielen die Künstler
nur auf die Liebe ab.*
Marsilio Ficino

Sein Rücken schmerzt, vielleicht ein Zeichen
des Endes, diese Schmerzen. Er hat diese
Rückenschmerzen und Fieber und seine Knie
sind lasch, man wird einen Arzt rufen müssen.
Lieber brächte er seine Arbeit zu Ende. Denn beeile
dich, sagte sie, seine Jugend, die gestern war.
Den Journalisten öffnet er die Tür (was er
sonst nie tat). Auf Frage, im Morgenmantel:
Ich komme mit dem Tod gut aus, ich werde
tot, ein unbeugsamer Toter sein. Das Delir
der Anfänge? Davon sagt sich nichts –
Es gab andere Leben und andere Frauen
und immer eine trunkene Abfahrt zum Meer.

Die Themen? Die Mechanik, die fürchterliche
Verletzlichkeit der Schwellen, Frauenrücken
(in einen ließ er Violinschlüssel ein), Spiel mit
Strahlen, mit Lippen, alles, was unermüdlich ist,
später zunehmende Blanc-de-Blanc-Heiterkeit,
Abschied von den Riesinnen, die Helden
an langen Leinen kirregeritten, Lirum, Larum,
doppeltrum, in jeder Schrift, auf zweiter Spur
trittst du ins warme Zimmer der Kindheit ein,
das ist die ganze Bühne, mit der Sonne
ein glühender Haufen Stein über dem Berg.

Den weißen Kamm des Bergs sieht er von seinem
Fenster jetzt. Schnee spiegelt sich in der See.
Neben ihm das Schachspiel, vor ihm der Tisch
mit einer Zeichnung von Seeigeln, grüne Asphodelen,
ein schönes, allein von den Händen geschmücktes
Gelände, aus dem er sich ungern entfernt. Vom
unablässigen Wind der Bilder sind seine Augen
blank, die rote Schleife paßt zum roten Garn,
der Hang zu Finessen und Licht ist geblieben.
Er hat gelebt, er besitzt das ganze Leben in der
Erinnerung. Südlichkeiten, Glücke um ein Nichts:

from *Sage ich zu wem*

Portrait of the artist as an old man

Moreover, artists aim at nothing other than love.
Marsilio Ficino

His back aches, perhaps a sign
of the end, these pains. He has these
pains in the back and is feverish, his knees
are slack, a doctor may have to be called.
He'd rather finish his work. Because hurry,
it said, his youth that was yesterday.
He opens the door to the journalists – something
he never did before. Questioned, in his dressing-gown,
I'm on good terms with death, declares, and, dead,
I shall be inflexible. The delirium
of beginnings? Of that I'll say nothing –
there were other lives and other women
and always a drunken escape to the sea.

His themes? The mechanics, the terrible
vulnerability of thresholds, women's backs
(into one he inserted a treble clef), a playing
with rays, with lips, with all that is indefatigable,
later a growing indifference or equanimity,
farewell to the giantesses, the heroes
broken in on their lunging-reins, hey diddle-diddle,
round and round, in every script, on the second track
you enter the warm room of childhood
that's the whole of the stage, with the sun
a glowing heap of rock above the mountain.

That mountain's white peak he sees now
from his window. The sea mirrors its snow.
Beside him the chessboard, before him the table
with a drawing of sea urchins, green asphodels,
a lovely tract enriched by his hands only
which he is loath to leave. His eyes are bright
with the incessant wind of pictures,
the red bow chimes with the red thread,
his taste for *finesses* and light has not left him.
He has lived, he possesses all of his life
in remembrance. Southerlinesses, joys about nothing,

from *To someone I say*

27

sie tragen ihn, die Trümmer tragen sich. Es
zählen Güte, Schönheit, eine freie Seele, Form.
Keine Sünde, die Toten zu überleben. Keine
Sünde, keine eigenen Gedanken zu haben.
Und die unermüdliche Liebe? Unermüdliche?
Unüberwindliche. Zwischen dem Ruhm und den jungen
Frauen, die ihn besuchen, ist eine Beziehung,
die er am Abend nicht mehr bestimmen kann.

from *Sage ich zu wem*

they bear him up, the ruins bear themselves up. They
count for him, goodness, beauty, a soul that's free, form.
It's not a sin to outlive one's dead. Not a
sin to have no thoughts of one's own.
And indefatigable love? Indefatigable?
No, inexpugnable. Between fame and the young
women who visit him there is a connection
which evening slithers beyond his grasp.

Michael Hamburger

from *To someone I say*

Der Tod von Manhattan

Vom Flugzeug:
Termitenbaum des späten Jahrtausends.
Das Gerät zeigt, wo er ragt,
zwischen zwei Flüssen
und gewaltigen Depots des Blicks.
Die alten Häuser wurden abgerissen,
Kurven und ihre Akazien begradigt.
So hoch sind in den gläsernen Türmen
die Mieten gestiegen, daß die Leute nach Queens
zogen und Williamsburg, Brooklyn,
mit Splittern ihrer phantastischen
privaten Visionen. Sie hatten nicht gelernt,
daß Ehrlichkeit eine Technik ist und die
Wahrheit sich heute nomadisch gibt,
in Mäandern gelegt um die Erschöpfung
des Herzens. Aber im *Hamburger Motel*
gibt's Brötchen frei, und die Prinzessinnen,
die sie immer erniedrigen wollten,
sind gerade erst 13 Jahre alt, weiß
wie das Fenstereis des Winters.

Der Tod ist die Kante des Raums, sagt der
Maler. So lebt jeder mit Blick über die Flüsse
auf den postutopischen Ort und versucht
sich im Echo dessen, was er erlebte.
Der Mond geht auf, du kannst jeden Krater
zwischen den Flugzeugen sehen, so klar
ist es. Und deine Geschichte neigt dazu,
ihre gladiatorische Haut abzuwerfen
und sich in sich hineinzufalten wie
ein geheimnisvolles Origami-Papier.

from *Sage ich zu wem*

The death of Manhattan

From the plane:
a termite tree as the chiliad ends.
The instruments show where it's jutting up
between two rivers
and the look's colossal deposits.
The old houses have been pulled down,
curves straightened, acacias and all.
The rents have risen so sky-high
in the glass towers that lodgers
have moved to Queens and Williamsburg, Brooklyn,
taking shards of their chimerical
private visions with them. They'd not learnt
that honesty is a technique and that truth
is posing as a nomad these days,
meandering around the exhaustion
of the heart. But bread rolls are free
in the Hamburger Motel, while the princesses
they always yearned to humiliate
have just turned thirteen, and are as white
as the ice on windows in wintertime.

Death is the edge of space, says the painter.
That's how everyone lives with a view across the rivers
towards the post-utopian city, practising
echoing what they have experienced.
The moon is rising: there's so much light
that you can make out every crater
between the planes. And your private history
is doing its best to slough off its gladiatorial skin
and fold itself into itself like
some kind of cryptic origami paper.

Richard Dove

Hellblau, mit Mond

Orhan Veli, nimm noch ein Schlückchen
dem Mond zuliebe,
nein, zu Ehren des Monds,
blaßgrüne Glühbirne
überm verschlammten Goldenen Horn,
die selbst das Geheul der Muezzine (18 Uhr 30)
nicht zu bersten vermag.

Dein Stein ist neben dem Stein von Tezer.
Wenn man schon ruhen muß,
ruht ihr am schönsten Ort:
unter altem Lorbeer
oberhalb des Bosporus
am Rumeli Hisar
unter einem Stein,
den wir sehen und hören.

Ihr sprecht zu euren Büchern in diesem Park.
Nicht anders könnt ihr erscheinen,
habt eurem Tod Sprache beigebracht
das kurze Leben lang.

Könntet ihr nur Istanbul sehen, jetzt,
von den Soldaten verlassen, für eine Weile,
schöner denn je,
die wehenden Alevimäntel
und 27 Minarette vom Café Pierre Loti –

noch ein Schlückchen, ach,
es ist kitschig hier,
hellblau, mit Mond,
und ernst, ernste Terrassen
mit Marmorzäunen im Quadrat
und das klagende Tambur von Ney.

Trinkt aus,
was weder Atem ist noch Mund.
Ihr könnt nicht anders erscheinen:
das Licht der Küsse im Blätterflackern
dieses Gartens.

Light blue, with moon

Drink, Orhan Veli, one more drop
for love of the moon,
no, in honour of the moon,
the pale green lightbulb
above the silted Golden Horn,
and even the muezzins howling
at six-thirty p.m.
have no power to shatter it.

Your stone is next to Tezer's.
If rest is necessary at all,
yours is the loveliest resting place,
beneath an old laurel tree,
above the Bosphorus,
close to Rumeli Hisar,
underneath a stone we see and hear.

In this park you both speak to your books.
You could appear no other way,
life in all its brevity spent
instructing your death in speech.

If only you could see, now, Istanbul,
abandoned for a while by the soldiers,
more beautiful than ever,
the Alevi robes fluttering
and the sight of twenty-seven minarets
from the Café Pierre Loti –

one drop more, ah
what a lot of kitsch hereabouts,
light blue, with moon,
and serious, the serious terraces,
and fences, squared, of marble,
and the flutist mournful with his ney.

Drink up neither breath nor mouth.
You could appear no other way:
the light of kisses
in this garden's flickering leaves.

Christopher Middleton

from
Der Tisch wird kalt
The table grows cold
(1992)

Eine Feige für den Heimweg

Die Pferde traben, eines kackt,
und Anna sagt: als würde
es Tomaten rauswerfen.
Es ist dieses Geräusch, und
der leichte Nebel des Sägemehls,
und zwischen den Planken
die Sonne, die wieder untergeht.
Die Polofrau hat ein sehr enges,
schwarzes Kostüm. Wir pflücken
uns aus der grünen Tüte
eine Feige für den Heimweg.

from *Der Tisch wird kalt*

A fig for the way home

The horses trot, one shits,
and Anna says: as if it would
throw out tomatoes.
It is this sound, and
the gentle fog of the sawdust,
and between the planks
the sun, that goes down again.
The polo woman has a very tight
black suit. We pick
for ourselves out of the green bag
a fig for the way home.

Sibylle Schlesier

Auf Annas Schreibtisch

Ein Kaktus, Recorder, Glanzbilder, Hefte,
eine dreidimensionale Zelle, selbstgebastelt
für den Bio-Unterricht mit Kern, Membrane,
das Zellwasser angedeutet mit blaßblauem
Papier. Das Ganze größer und wuchtiger
als unterm Mikroskop, das sonst doch
für Magie Sorge trägt. Die Zeit ist langsam,
in der alles auf diesem Tisch existiert:
die Comics, Kassetten, Ohrringe, Stifte.
Die Zeit ist still. Das Gegenteil seiner
Besitzerin. Sie muß den anderen mitteilen,
was sie entdeckt. Die Stimme führt zum Ton.
Zwischen den Tönen, dem Sternenkatalog
auf dem Tisch läuft ein Band zu dem Glas,
das sie zum Brief faltet vor dem Schlaf.
Nicht wie bei uns, von allen Richtungen
kommt die Zeit auf das Kind.

from *Der Tisch wird kalt*

On Anna's writing table

A cactus, recorder, glossy pictures, notebooks,
a three-dimensional cell cobbled together
for her bugs course with nucleus, membrane,
the cell water hinted at via pale blue
paper. The whole thing's bigger, more weighty,
than under the microscope which usually
works the magic. Slow the time
in which all things exist on this table:
the comics, cassettes and earrings and pens.
Time keeps still. The opposite of this
table's owner. She must tell the others
what she's discovered. The voice leads to the sound.
Between the sounds, the catalogue of stars
on the table a tape runs to the glass
she folds into a letter prior to sleep.
Not as in our case, from all directions
time dawns on the child.

Richard Dove

from *The table grows cold*

Einem Delphin in Batumi

Ein Erinnerer geht am Strand,
übers Gekugel der schwarzen Steine.
Einst war es anders, sagten alle.
So sagt er: Nein, zum Fotografen
mit dem Holzdelphin,
zeig mir noch einen,
der hier lebt,
und ich lasse mich bannen.
Reglos, derweil,
stehen sie am Wasserrand
und schauen hinaus.

Nach Tagen, nach Jahren
räumen sie den schnittigen Kadaver
fort.

from *Der Tisch wird kalt*

To a dolphin in Batumi

A man walks along the beach, remembering,
over rolling black pebbles.
It used to be different, they all said.
So he says: No, to the photographer
with the wooden dolphin,
show me a single
live one here
and I'll let you take me.
Motionless, meanwhile,
they stand by the water's edge
and look out.

Days, years later,
they remove the streamlined
cadaver.

Rosmarie Waldrop

Stambul

Heruntergekommen
sieht der Mond aus
durch das lange Rohr
auf wackligem Stativ,
aufgestellt am Rand des Taksim-Platzes,
aber der Blick kostet nur 500 Lira,
der Mann dreht an Rädern,
du beugst dich über eine kleine Linse
und siehst ihn, nah,
weiß und kühl, Krater und Täler,
selbst den schwarzen Fleck de beauté –
heruntergekommen etwas,
aber nicht halb so schäbig und wirklich
wie der Taksim mit seinem Verkehr,
den verwelkten Büchern auf staubigen Ständern
und klingelnden Mandelverkäufern.
Du gehst in den Menschen über den Platz.
Die Oleanderbüsche stehen
in ihrem runden Schatten
unter dem Neonlicht.
Der Mond ist klein, eine helle Scheibe
ohne Relief im Dunst der Sommernacht.
Nur du weißt, wie er aussieht,
ohne Leben,
präzis weiß und kühl, fast blau.

from *Der Tisch wird kalt*

Stamboul

It looks run down,
the moon does,
seen through the long tube
on a wobbly mount
set up on the edge of Taksim Square,
but it costs only five hundred lira to look,
the man gives the wheels a turn,
you stoop to a small lens
and see it close,
white and cool, craters and valleys,
even the black beauty spot,
a bit run down
but not half so shabby and real
as Taksim and its traffic,
its wilted books on dusty shelves
and bell-ringing almond-vendors.
You walk across the square among people.
Underneath the neon light
the oleander bushes stand
in their circular shadows.
The moon is small, a featureless
shining disk in the summer night haze.
You alone know how it looks,
lifeless,
precisely white and cool, almost blue.

Christopher Middleton

Venedig

Die Lagune beharrt auf ihrer Grenze.
Keine Autoreifen, die im Regen dampfen.
Die Kranken mit Blaulicht
auf blauen Booten kutschiert.
Statt Pound finden wir Sonia
auf dem Cimetero San Michele,
junge Frau aus grüner Bronze,
ruhend auf rotem Porphyr,
Chignon und aufgeworfene Brüste,
unweit von Stravinsky und Diaghilev.
Eine *adoratrice* hat Spitzenschuhe
an den Schalenfuß gebunden.

Ein Meer künstlicher Blumen
wie zu süßliche Worte:
zum Einreißen und Verstreuen
auf der versauten Lagune.

from *Der Tisch wird kalt*

Venice

Doggedly, the lagoon insists upon its confines.
No car-tyres steaming in the rain.
The sick get driven by in blue boats
whose blue lamps are flashing.
Instead of Pound we find Sonia there
in the Cimetero San Michele –
a young woman fashioned out of green bronze
reposing on red porphyry,
her hair in a chignon, with upraised breasts,
not far from Stravinsky, Diaghilev.
An *adoratrice* has tied ballet shoes
to the foot of the vessel.

An ocean of artificial flowers
like too sugary words:
fit to be torn up, scattered
across the contaminated lagoon.

Richard Dove

from *The table grows cold*

Abermärchen glauben

Ich höre seine Stimme
lege meine Fingernägel
in die Rille den Nagel
die Stimme von dem
der unter dem schwarzen Ast
in die Seine ging
der den Rückzug durchsuchte
Rose und Licht und Asche
und ihr Allerschrecklichstes
Rauch   Und der riet
Abermärchen zu glauben
und der nicht wußte
wenn er die Maulstücke würgte
ob es das Innere seines Mundes
oder das Herz ihrer Körper war
und der riet unverhohlen
die eigenen Lippen zu röntgen
der Liebesnahme einen Gesang
zu setzen so zum Ende
im vorvorletzten warmen Haus

from *Der Tisch wird kalt*

Believing in make-believe tales

I hear his voice
lay my finger-nails
in the groove the nail
the voice of him
who under the black branch
went into the Seine
who searched the way back
rose and light and ashes
and most dreadful of all
smoke   And who advised
belief in make-believe tales
and who did not know
when he gulped down those mouthings
whether it was the inside of his mouth
or the heart of their bodies
and who advised undisguisedly
to X-ray one's own lips
to set for sole voices
the taking-away of love
and so to the end
in the last warm house before the last but one

Michael Hamburger

from *The table grows cold*

Monate

September, Durst, kürzere Tage, Reue.
Dezember, Regen.
Vom August ein Foto: Paar (zwei), 2 Kinder,
Statisten, liegt weiter zurück.
Auf der anderen Seite des Blatts beginnt der Tag.
Keine Blätter im Januar, kein Tag,
der sich nicht gliche.
Die roten Vorhänge mit ihrem Licht für Exzesse
(die es nicht gab) schaben über die Fensterbank
in der warmen Brise. Nachts
gibt es keine Nacht, nur Sterne,
eins zwei drei vier: die Deichsel.
Und vier: der Wagen, der große Wagen,
aus dem sich Funken lösen. Du
schreibst alles auf einem blauen Tisch.
Das ist das Wasser, der Himmel, der
früheste Morgen (ohne Wein und Musik).
Das ist das Brett des Gebets, des Versagens.
Es gibt keine Flügel wie Sinn.
März. Im März bist du geboren.
Im April wirst du davonjagen
auf dem Bretterwagen.

from *Der Tisch wird kalt*

The months

September, thirst, the shortening days, remorse.
December, rain.
From August, a photograph: a pair (two), two children,
extras, out of the distance.
On the further side of a leaf the day begins.
No leaves in January, no day
not the same.
The red curtains with their light of excess
(although nothing happened) scrape on the windowsill
in the warm breeze. Nights
without night, only stars,
one two three four: the Shaft.
And four: the Great Car, the Carriage,
with its sparks loosened. You
write always at a blue table.
It is the water, the heavens, the
earliest morning (lacking wine and music).
It is the board of prayer, of failure.
There is no meaning, to bring us wings.
March. In March you were born.
In April you will stand upon
the planks of the Chariot, and will be gone.

Robert Gray

from *The table grows cold*

(die Liebe)

Auch das Haus, wie alles, wird geboren
und zerspringt und stirbt. Selbst die Geschichte
der Quellen belegt es, und der Fluß strömt
ins Meer, bis er nicht mehr ist. Überflutet.
Wie wir in einem fort überredet werden
und uns vergeblich anlegen mit den Rednern.
Die Schwärze übersetzt uns zurück
durch ihr scheinendes Sieb. Mit Augen,
gut repariert, und hartherzigem Herzen
gehen wir durch Klagemauern, Steh-
aufmännchen in der Wachaufnacht.
Etwas, das alles vor uns niedergewälzt
und planiert hat (die Liebe), steht
schweißkalt jetzt in der Ecke,
zernagt und hart wie Kaurigeld.
Wir kaufen damit keine Freuden.
Nur die Luft über der feuchten Haut
leuchtet, ein schwaches Feuerwerk
am Ende der Schönheit.

from *Der Tisch wird kalt*

(love)

The house, too, like everything, is born
and explodes and dies. Even the history
of the wells proves it, and the river streams
into the sea, until it no longer is. Awash.
As we are incessantly persuaded
and get into futile fights with these talkers.
Darkness transports us back
through its suggestive sieve. With eyes
well repaired, and hard-hearted heart
we go through wailing walls, tumbler-
doll in the waking night.
Something, that has rolled over and leveled
everything before us (love), stands
in a cold sweat now in the corner,
gnawed and hard as a cowry shell.
We don't buy any pleasures with it.
Only the air over the damp skin
glows, weak fireworks
at the end of beauty.

Sibylle Schlesier

from *The table grows cold*

Der Sphinx

Das auf 150 Tonnen geschätzte Haupt
darf nicht stürzen doch
reißt der Kalkstein und stürzt
in sanfter
an beiden Flanken
eingerüsteter Schläfrigkeit
an den rostbraunen Nippeln
vorbei
ins blühende Salz
der Zementfugen dort
wo Halit und Gips
die alten Steine wehklagen lassen
von Geburt krankheitsanfällig
das Plateau erschüttert dazu
von den gewaltigen Bussen der Horden:
da hilft kein gutes Achten mehr.
Aber niemand verliert viel
beim Verträpfeln
wie Länder und Städte
in die Ferne schwinden
und der Brösler ohne Rätsel
endlich fällt.

from *Der Tisch wird kalt*

The Sphinx

Estimated at 150 tons, the head
mustn't fall but
limestone cracks and falls
past
rust-brown nipples
scaffolded
on both flanks
with gentle sleepiness
into the thriving salt
of cement joints
where halite and plaster
make old stones complain
prone from birth to illness
the plateau shudders too
with the thunderous busses of the hordes:
no more great regard helps here.
But nobody loses much
during the dripping away
as countries and cities
vanish into the distance
and the crumbler without riddles
finally falls.

Andrew Shields

from *The table grows cold*

Vorgespräch über Fragment

Ruini parlanti
Piranesi

Der Innenraum spricht zu uns,
deutlicher als die Kohorten,
die schreiend an Stricken
Quader hochzerrten
ins Unermeßliche,
das es ja nicht gibt.
Das es nicht gibt:
Der Turm bleibt Fragment,
die Schreie verstummt,
Serpentinen geebnet,
Libretto schlecht.
Hörst du?

Bab-ili? Unhörbar:
ein Regen toter Federn.

from *Der Tisch wird kalt*

Preliminary conversation about fragments

Ruini parlanti
Piranesi

The interior speaks to us,
more clearly than the cohorts
who, screaming, dragged
the blocks up, on ropes,
into the boundless
which of course does not exist.
Which does not exist:
The tower remains a fragment,
the screams fallen silent,
the serpentines made plain,
bad libretto.
You hear me?

Bab-ili? Inaudible:
rain of dead feathers.

Rosmarie Waldrop

Abdo Rimbo

Am 10. Dezember 1878
schenkte man dem Verstockten,
dem Abgebrannten einen
schwarzen Sonnenschirm
mit grünem Futter.
Er suchte Arbeit,
fand keine (und keine
beim britisch-ägyptischen Zoll),
schlief im haarigen Haus,
die Betteljugend im Puls,
vergessen, verachtet, stark.
Das war in Alexandria,
einer Stadt, deren einzige Uhr
das Meer war, träge und
diodenrot bei den Felsen.

Es gibt *Besseres*, immer, *anderswo*.
So suchte er ein Schiff
mit Segeln, einen ‚Sambuk'.
In Aden Town (Mitte 1884)
nimmt er eine Frau.
Die Äthioperin ist mehr *Idee*,
eine der *Formeln* für das Heil,
Frau von roter Haut.

Er läßt sie unterrichten
in der französischen Sprache,
‚Le Magasin Pittoresque'
ihr Lehrmittel,
dieser nègre blanc!
Er lernt Amharisch,
Gaflah: die Karawane.
Handelt mit rostigen
belgischen Gewehren (was
umstritten ist), verzweifelt
von jedem Punkt der Welt.

from *Der Tisch wird kalt*

Abdo Rimbo

On 10 December 1878
they gave him, unrepentant fellow,
burnt-out case that he was,
a black parasol
with a green lining.
He was looking for work,
finding none (and none
with Anglo-Egyptian customs),
sleeping in that wretched house,
his beggarly youth throbbing on his pulse,
forgotten, despised, strong.
That was in Alexandria,
a city whose only timepiece
was the sea, idle and
diode-red by the rocks.

There's *something better*, always, *somewhere else*.
So he went looking for a ship,
a sailing-boat, a sambuk.
In Aden Town (mid 1884)
he took himself a woman,
Abyssinian, more an *idea*,
one of the *formulae* for salvation,
a woman red of skin.

He had her given lessons
in the French language,
'Le Magasin Pittoresque'
her textbook,
this *nègre blanc*!
He learned Amharic,
gaflah: a caravan.
Traded rusty
Belgian guns (this
is disputed), despaired
at every point in the world.

Michael Hulse

Aus dem Glossar der Prostitution in Algier

Aufrecht im Arian
Bandmaster und Begum
couill'-à-cul
estoc fado
klaren klagenden Kopfes
fissa fissa kouça
Locken aus falschem Jet
mignott' auf 'scheuertem
Linoleum nubile Töchter
des Aurès
Hennahände
um den Knochen rot:
Ouallah Biskra point' buic
Ouled Nail Gide
valseur wellfed
le chien
pesant: rhlass!

from *Der Tisch wird kalt*

From the glossary of prostitution in Algiers

Upright in the Arian
bandmaster and begum
couill'-à-cul
estoc fado
with a clear complaining head
fissa fissa kouça
locks pseudo-jet black
mignott' on scrubbed
linoleum nubile daughters
of Aurès
henna hands
red round the bone:
Ouallah Biskra point' buic
Ouled Nail Gide
valseur well-fed
le chien
pesant: rhlass!

Maccaronic Montage

from *The table grows cold* 59

Kleine Königin der schönen Huren

an Juan Carlos Onetti

I

Die Adventssterne blinken
in den Fenstern des ‚Eldorado'.
Sie bleibt in Strümpfen, ich
im Hemd. Wir tun es mir, ihr,
uns. Beim Hinausgehen
sehe ich die Spuren
der Pfennigabsätze
im Türholz, in Kniehöhe.
Es ist Nacht. Es regnet.
Die Schnecken atmen
an den Botschaftsmauern
im Tiergarten. Einer
grölt von Einheit
und Geld.

II

Ich geh' nach Venezuela,
hat sie gesagt (mit diesen langen,
zweideutigen Schritten), und meine
Kamera ist kaputt. Es gibt keine
Reparatur an der erinnerten
Nation, hab' ich gesagt,
steck dir
die Filmkerze ins Aug'.
So lassen wir uns bräunen,
so gut's der späte Winter
kann. Doch niemand,
sagt sie, klaut mir
meine Nacht.

from *Der Tisch wird kalt*

Little queen of the beautiful whores

to Juan Carlos Onetti

I

Advent stars blink
in the windows of the 'Eldorado'.
She keeps her hose on, I,
my shirt. We do it to me, her,
us. Leaving
I see traces
of stiletto heels
on the door frame, knee high.
It is night. It is raining.
Snails breathe
along the embassy walls
in Tiergarten. Someone
bawls about unity
and money.

II

I'm going to Venezuela,
she said (with those long,
ambiguous steps), and my
camera's broken. There is no
repairing the nation we
remember, I said,
put a
film candle in your eye.
We'll get a tan,
the best late winter
can come up with. But no one,
she says, is going to rip off
my night.

from *The table grows cold*

III

Im Theater der Sensiblen
war eine Unruhe lang Liebe.
Dann neigte sich die schnelle Stunde
des zerfahrnen Samstags
in den Abend.
Flashback: Ich schau dir
zu. Du hältst dich zu.
Adieu, auf bald. Immer
ist die Angst der Trick
der Voyeure.

from *Der Tisch wird kalt*

III

In the theater of the sensitive
there was love for the space of an unrest.
Then the quick hour
of a Saturday driven to pieces sagged
into evening.
Flashback: I hold you in
sight. You hold yourself shut.
Adieu. So long. Always,
fear is a trick
of voyeurs.

Rosmarie Waldrop

Ratschlag zum Verzehr der Auster

Es genügt aber auch
ein einfaches Taschenmesser
mit starker kurzer Klinge
zum Öffnen

wenn du ungeübt bist
nimm ein Tuch
um dich nicht zu verletzen
Die Messerspitze

schiebst du
an der dicksten Seite
am Schließmuskel
zwischen die beiden Schalenhälften

den Deckel brichst du ab
die Schalensplitter entfernst du
aber niemals das Wasser
das du dem Fleisch hinterher

schlürfen mußt
Austern die sich von selbst
öffnen solltest du
nicht verzehren

Mit dem Wasser trinkst du
die Schreie der Krabben
den Schatten der Wellen
und den Strudel am Grund

Mit dem Fleisch kaust du
auf der Liebe   Sie läßt
nicht mehr los als gäbe
es dort zu graben

nach Vorteilen und Schrecken
und ein Kummer wächst in dir
der dein Leben begleitet
und währt es noch so lang

from *Der Tisch wird kalt*

Advice on how to eat oysters

But a simple pocket-knife
with a strong short blade
is also enough
to prise them open

if you're unpractised
take a cloth
so as not to injure yourself
The tip of the knife

you should push
at the thickest place
into the sphincter
between the two halves of the shell

you break off the lid
remove the splinters of shell
don't lose the water
which you must slurp

after eating the meat
Oysters that open of their
own accord you
should not consume

With the water you're drinking
the shrieks of crabs
the shadow of waves
and the swirl across the sea-floor

With the meat you're chewing
on love   You won't be left
loose for long
to delve there after

advantages and terrors
a kind of grief appears
that will go with you now all your life
whatever score is added to you

Robert Gray

Rauhreifuhr

Allein auf der Erdkruste, erdgrau,
bunte Patronenhülsen auf eichgrauen Wegen,
von einem Strahl Sonne durchquert:
Und plötzlich ist Abend. Harzwasser
tropft immer noch aus dem Nußbaum.
Was für ein Jahr!
‚Runder als das O des Giotto',
also träger, müßiger, trauriger.
Als was? Nicht das sinnlose
Schwenken der Fahnen, die Wippe
der Zeit, das Öffnen des Tors.
Nicht der gutgemeinte Rat:
‚Zerr Winterfeigen vom grauen Ast.'
Der Reif geht mit dem Schatten zur Mauer.
Jetzt setzt sich die rotgoldne Landschaft
über alle Staffage hinweg und dunkelt,
und ich, nach all dem Herumgehen
und Schauen und den Stunden am Radio,
zieh mir die kalte Uhr übers Gelenk
und fange zu schreiben an:
‚Mit dem Schatten ging der Reif zur Mauer.'

(1.1.1990, Sicellino)

from *Der Tisch wird kalt*

Hoarfrostwatch

Alone on the crust of the earth, earth-gray,
motley cartridge cases on oak-gray paths
crossed by a ray of sun:
And suddenly night. Resin
drops from the walnut tree.
What a year!
'Rounder than the O in Giotto,'
hence lazier, more idle, sadder.
Than what? Not the senseless
waving of flags, the seesaw
of time, the opening of the gate.
Not the well-meant advice:
'Wrench winter figs off the gray branch.'
Hoarfrost, in the shade, reaches the wall.
Now the goldred landscape
slights all decor and grows dark,
and I, after all this walking
and looking and hours by the radio,
pull the cold watch over my wrist
and start writing.
'In the shade, hoarfrost reached the wall.'

(1.1.1990, Sicellino)

Rosmarie Waldrop

In dieser schwarzen Ruhe

Poetry is a destructive force
Wallace Stevens

Der feine Staub des Vergessens
weht über dich, über die Baustelle,
du bist die Baustelle,
du siebst den Sand,
willst etwas raussieben
aus ihm, aus den Körnchen:
ein totes Gras, eine Versteinerung,
den Farn der alten Liebe,
für immer unscharf, bröselnd,
selbst im erinnerten Licht
der viel zu vielen Worte,
als sei der Spiegel sehr groß
und sein Gegenstand sehr klein,
kein Ruhmesblatt, ein Winziges,
eine Staubritze,
ein geädertes Stimmgras war's,
das jetzt auf Schleichwegen wieder
auf dich zuzittert, immer umsonst,
für immer rätselhaftes parlando,
gestanzt und flau:

,Was macht man mit diesen störenden Händen?'
,Man verschränkt sie. Faltet sie.'
,Ist's ein Ruhender oder – ?'
,Wenn du nur den Fährlohn hast',
sagt die mit dem kleinen roten Kreuz
über dem Gesicht. (Ihre Haut
war aus Blättern. Du siebst
nach diesen Blättern.) Schließlich
setzen wir über, mitten im Gespräch.
Wir sind da. Der große Spiegel glänzt.
Die Klänge verhallen.
Die Blumen sind schwer und grün.
Sie welken. Das Glas funkelt.
Die Gläser stürzen hin und brechen.
Dem steht bis zur Eichel der Schlamm.
Ein letztes Mal flattern die Schmetterlinge auf.
Das Brot vertrocknet. Die Uhr ist zerlegt.

from *Der Tisch wird kalt*

In this black stillness

Poetry is a destructive force
Wallace Stevens

Fine oblivion dust
drifts over you, on the building site,
this site is you,
you sift the sand,
want to sift something
out of it, out of the grains:
dead grass, a fossil,
the fern of the old love,
for ever blurred, crumbling,
even in recollected light
of the excessive words,
as if the mirror were too large
its object very small,
no great credit to fame,
tiny, a dust crack,
veined grass of intonations
that now again in secret ways
trembles toward you, always in vain,
for every enigmatical parlando,
confessed, indifferent:

'What to do with these obtrusive hands?'
'One folds them. Clasps them.'
'Is it someone at rest or – ?'
'If you only have the ferry coin,'
says the one with a small red cross
over her face. (Her skin
was of leaves. You sift
for these leaves.) Finally
we cross, at the heart of speech.
There we are. The great mirror shines.
Sounds become fainter.
Flowers are heavy and green.
They wilt. Glass sparkles.
Glasses fall down and break.
He stands up to his glans in mud.
One last time butterflies flutter.
Bread dries up. The clock is taken apart.

from *The table grows cold*   69

Die Haut verliert ihren Glanz.
Die Liebe ist dort, sie wird gehalten.
Sie schwirrt empor.
Ihre Lebhaftigkeit ist nichts als Verfall.
Die Blätter sind kräftig an dicken Stauden.
Ihr Saft sichert aus Schwären.
‚In einem solchen Fall', sagt der Fremden-Prospekt,
‚empfiehlt sich der Rückzug ins Helle.'
Doch wollen wir bleiben. In dieser schwarzen Ruhe.
Es bleiben uns die Worte.
Die rohen, die haltbaren Worte
schwirren aus dem kenternden Boot.

‚…blutet die Falte' ‚Sie blutet mit grauen Lippen'
‚Verkeilst dich warum sing doch frei
unter der Bluse ein Blick' Bissig: ‚rate mal'
‚Weißt du die Farbe? Und ist es
dieses grüne Grau wie du?'
‚Von altem Farn?' Betäubt?
Wir stellen das Geleier der Lautsprecher ab.
Die Neonstangen fliehen durch Glas
in den nächtlichen Himmel,
ein Gewirr sehr heller Linien,
das dichter und blasser wird. Hier, vor dir,
dunkelt die Baustelle ohne Maß, bekränzt,
begrenzt von Brettern und Ende.
Im Zimmer dann wäschst du dich,
in jeder Hand eine kleine Hotelseife,
bis auf die neuen Nerven hinab.
Dein Fund: ein Dorn, ein zartes Lid
und zartere Knochen, ein Draht,
ein Spielzeuggewitter in Stein.
Geäder darin wie Pisse von Lurchen.

Im nächtlichen *charnier* waren
drei Reihen Schienbeine, so leicht,
eine Reihe Schädel; kunstvoll geschichtet,
freigegeben von einem gesättigteren
anderen Erdreich (einst)
wie im Auge verscharrte
billige Blicke,
aufgetan,
– getaut.

The skin loses its shine.
Love is there. She is embraced.
She buzzes upward.
Her liveliness is nothing but decay.
The leaves are strong on thick bushes.
Their sap oozes from sores.
'In such a case,' says the tourist leaflet,
'retreat to clarity is recommended.'
Yet we will stay. In this black stillness.
We are left with the words.
The raw, the lasting words
buzz out of the capsizing boat.

'...bleeds the fold' 'It bleeds with gray lips'
'Wedge yourself tight why not though sing freely
glance under blouse' Penetrating: 'guess'
'You know the color? Is it
the same gray green like you?'
'Of ancient fern?' Stunned?
We turn the droning blare of speakers off.
The neon tubes escape through glass
into the nocturnal sky,
an entanglement of very bright lines,
becoming denser and paler. Here, before you,
the building site grows immeasurably dark, crowned,
confined by boards and an end.
in the room then you wash yourself,
in each hand a small hotel soap,
down to the new nerves.
Your find: a thorn, a delicate lid
and more delicate bones, a wire,
a toy-storm in stone.
Veins therein like toad piss.

In the nocturnal *charnier*
three rows of shin-bones, so light,
a row of skulls; artfully layered,
released from a more saturated
different ground (once)
like cheap glances secretly
buried in the eye,
opened up,
– thawed.

from *The table grows cold*   71

Im nächtlichen Atelier:
Pinsel, ein Arsenal von Formen, ein Sieb,
Haar, Schachtel, Kübel, Sarkophag,
der Abguß Pascals auf Steinwayschwarz.
Doch kannst und kannst und kannst und
kannst du sie nicht zusammensetzen:
nicht mit Faden, dem Leim, dem Stein aus ihrem Schoß,
den Ziffern der Daten, dem Draht, dem Staub,
du siebst den Staub, siebst ihn
zu ihrer Stimme auf dem Band,
die allerstarrsten Lippen.
Charnier von *chair*?
Ja, sie gab dir anfangs ihren Rücken,
so daß du sie nicht sahst. Dann:
War sie da, ganz, wie sonst nie.
Ein zweites heißes Sehen. Und:
Ihre Stimme, winzig, aus dieser Ritze:
‚Wer denn liebt mir?' und
alle Augenbisse kehrten wieder,
die Äderchen, Gerinnsel, Blut
(nur durch die Stimme: Blut),
und Blätterhaut, und Blätt...
...ein Bett aus grauen Blättern...
Ja, schwirrend, stotternd
breiten wir uns aus, schwach
wie wir sind, und nutzen die Situationen:
werfen absinkende Wolken
auf eine Wand für Himmelfahrt,
oder verschieben und versetzen uns
wie Worte auf langmütigem Papier.
Zum Ende dann: ‚Es war
nicht so gemeint.'

Traust wem da, Auge, schau:

Nulla figura im schwarzen Sieb.
Sieb dich nicht fort.

from *Der Tisch wird kalt*

In the nocturnal studio:
paintbrush, an arsenal of forms, a sieve,
hair, box, pail, sarcophagus,
Pascal's casting on Steinway black.
Yet you can and can and can and
can not put her together:
not with thread, the clay, the stone out of her womb,
the numbers of the dates, the wire, the dust,
you sift the dust, sift it
to her voice on the tape,
the most rigid lips.
Charnier from *chair*?
Yes, in the beginning she gave you her back,
so that you did not see her. Then:
she was there, completely, not as usual.
A second burning look. And:
her voice, tiny, from this crack:
'Who then loves mine?' and
all eye-bites turned again,
the little veins, clots, blood
(only through the voice, blood),
and leafy skin and leaf…
…a bed of gray leaves…
Yes, buzzing, stammering
we spread out, weak
as we are, and use the circumstances:
project some sinking clouds
onto a wall for an ascension,
or move, displace ourselves
like words on indulgent paper.
To the ending then: 'It wasn't meant
like that.'

Trust whom there? Eye, behold:

Nulla figura in the black sieve.
Don't sift yourself away.

Sibylle Schlesier and Nathaniel Tarn

from *The table grows cold*   73

from
Keiner gefriert anders
No one freezes differently
(1996)

La cigarette obligatoire

Du kommst am Abend,
du bittest mich, etwas zu tun.
Ich tue es, von dir besessen,
deinem Bild besetzt.
Ich gebrauche meine Augen,
nehme dich langsam,
um dich tiefer
unters Glas der Erinnerung
zu pressen. Der Fernseher
vor der goldenen Gitane
läuft fort.

from *Keiner gefriert anders*

La cigarette obligatoire

You come in the evening.
You ask me to do something.
I do it, obsessed with you,
occupied by your image.
I use my eyes,
take you slowly,
to press you deeper
beneath the glass
of memory. The TV set
in front of the golden Gitane
keeps running.

Michael Hulse

Gräber

Von hier in den Norden sind die Wege
trocken. Gelbes Gras,
Durst in den Wurzeln. Im Herzen.
Alles ist einfach, aber falsch.

Wenn ich versuche, Geschichte zu denken,
die riesigen Wirbelknochen
des Sauriers hinter den Blutbuchen
in der Invalidenstraße,
Bismarck in Marmor,
und Benn, ein Klingelschild in der Bozener, leblos.

In den Tiefen der Bunker
des Potsdamer Platzes in Berlin
liegen die Hufeisen von Hitlers Lieblingspferd.
Profile der Macht: Harnisch und Helm.
In der Hosentasche zerknicken wir
die Standarten. Voll Genugtuung
hören wir die Fahnen splittern
im Dunkel des Stoffs.

Vergeßt nicht die gefälschten Würfel der Dichter.
Wenn die Eisernen wieder herrschen,
werden wir uns trösten müssen,
Steine schmücken mit kleinen Steinen,
mit Wasser das Herz.

from *Keiner gefriert anders*

Graves

From here into the north, the ways are
dry. Yellow grass,
thirst in the roots. In the hearts.
It's all simple, but false.

When I try to think history,
the enormous vertebrae
of the dinosaur behind the purple beeches
in Invalidenstraße,
Bismarck in marble,
and Benn, a nameplate on Bozener, lifeless.

In the depths of the bunkers
on Potsdamer Platz in Berlin
are the shoes of Hitler's favorite horse.
Profile of power: armor and helmet.
In our pants pockets, we crumple
the banners. Full of satisfaction
we hear the flags splinter
in the fabric's darkness.

Don't forget the poets' loaded dice.
When iron rules again,
we will have to console ourselves,
adorn stones with smaller stones,
the heart with water.

Andrew Shields

from *No one freezes differently*

Eine Fotografie von J.P. (1964)

Es ist alles eine Frage des Gleichgewichts
zwischen den großen steinernen Häusern,
zwischen dem Tageshaus und dem Haus der Nacht.
Nichts ist verschiedener von einem Denkmal.
Die Bedrohung. Die über die Knochen
gezogene Wangenhaut. Das Runzelkorn.
Es gab keine *kleine sonnige Zeit,*
kein Entkommen. Die Nacht fällt.
Das Nachthaus ist schrecklich, das Haus
des Tages ist poetisch, ist leicht.
Ist Poesie leicht? licht? Bricht
sie ins Nachthaus geschmirgelt
von leuchtenden Zungen? Nicht
Abwehr im Blick. Nicht Augen.
Die Augen schauen an dir vorbei.
Im Entsetzen altert die Wahrheit schlechter.
Das ist ein Fluch. Ich weiß es
von der Seine.

from *Keiner gefriert anders*

A photograph of J.P. (1964)

It's all a question of balance
between the huge stone houses –
the house of day and the house of night.
Nothing resembles a monument less.
The menace. The skin of his cheeks
stretched across the bones. The reticulation grain.
There was no *little sunny spell*,
no getting away. The night is falling.
Night's house is loathsome, the house
of day is poetic, light.
Is poetry light? Limpid? Does it break
into night's house abrasively ground
by lustrous tongues? That
look parries nothing. No eyes.
The eyes are looking past you.
Truth ages less gracefully shone on by horror.
That is a curse. I know it
from the Seine.

Richard Dove

from *No one freezes differently*

Im Vernichtungsbuch

Daß die Bäcker ihre weißen Hände ausziehen.
Daß die Metzger vor den Tieren sterben.
Daß die Dichter einen nutzlosen Mund haben,
den sie rund machen und breit ziehen.
Das steht im Vernichtungsbuch geschrieben.

Nicht eingetragen
sind der Statuen durchlöcherte Sohlen,
dort, wo die Bleisockel in die Bronze griffen.
Daß man durch das fehlende Auge,
durch ein Loch im Schädel
zu den Ablagerungen im Inneren gelangte.
Daß die Werkzeuge bis in den Brustkorb reichten.
Daß sie dort eine Kugel fanden
von der Größe eines getrockneten Herzens.
Daß die Stempelkissen ihre Tinte verströmten,
das Papier schwärzten, alle Farben schluckten.

from *Keiner gefriert anders*

In the book of annihilation

That the bakers remove their white hands.
That the butchers perish before their animals.
That the poets have futile mouths
which they make rotund and stretch out to long-windedness.
That's all been written up in the book of annihilation.

What's not been recorded
are the undersides of the statues, perforated
where the lead plinths have encroached on the bronze.
That they got to the deposits inside
through the missing eye,
through a hole in the skull.
That the tools obtruded as far as the rib cage.
That they came across a sphere there
the size of a dried-up heart.
That the stamp-pads shed their ink,
made the paper black, swallowed all colours.

Richard Dove

from *No one freezes differently*

Alexandria: Ein Zyklus

Black, black, and be sure of it.
There is little sure.

Clark Coolidge, At Egypt

Hinter der alexandrinischen Bibliothek

An der Wand der Billardhalle
der Fleck noch vom Haar des jungen Mannes
mit den Hüften eines Akrobaten,
den der Dichter liebte und dessen
Untreue er bedeutungslos empfand
wie die Säule des Pompejus.
Eifersucht war 5 Minuten brauner, übermüdeter Regen
vor dem Perlenvorhang, ein alexandrinischer
Ausbruch von Apathie im schwachen Wind
über dem Mareotis-See.
Dessen Krododil, eine Mumie jetzt,
Hauptattraktion des griech.-röm. Museums,
streckt sich auf seinem Holzbett aus,
stichig verschuppt zu saurem Pulver:
nicht wirklich, haltbar.

from *Keiner gefriert anders*

Alexandria: A cycle

Black, black, and be sure of it.
There is little sure.

Clark Coolidge, *At Egypt*

Behind the Alexandrian Library

On the pool hall wall
still a hair-oil stain from
the young guy with acrobat hips
whom the Poet loved and whose
whoring bothered him as little
as Pompey's pillar.
Jealousy was five minutes of brown, sluggish rain
outside the bead curtain, an Alexandrian
outbreak of apathy in slack wind
over Lake Mareotis.
Whose crocodile, a mummy now –
main attraction of the Gr.-Rom. Museum –
stretches on its wooden bed,
scales blighted to acid dust:
not real, but lasting.

Rosmarie Waldrop

Alexandria

Dort hinten saß er, an diesem Marmortisch,
sagte der alte Kellner, unter den altmodischen Ventilatoren,
die sich damals schon träge drehten,
unter dieser Decke, Stuck des Art Nouveau,
la vie était confortable: Stanley Beach,
Glymenopoulo, und das anmutige
kleine Zizinia, ein Kino heute,
wo in der Saison Tosca gespielt wurde,
La Bohème und Lohengrin (das Strengste
von Wagner, das damals südlich von Neapel
akzeptierbar war). Dort saß er, ein Grieche
von ein paar zehntausend Griechen,
der eine halbe Million Ägypter nicht wahrnahm.
Er lebte in einem imaginären Europa,
stehengeblieben bei Strabo: ‚das großartigste
Emporium in der bewohnten Welt',
das jetzt aus Steinen ist und der See
und einem Gefühl der allergrößten Erschöpfung.

from *Keiner gefriert anders*

Alexandria

Back there is where he used to sit, that marble table,
said the old waiter, under the antiquated ceiling fans
that turned sluggishly even then,
under this ceiling with Art Nouveau stucco,
la vie était confortable: Stanley Beach,
Glymenopoulo, and the graceful
little Zizinia, a movie house now,
where they used to play Tosca in season,
La Bohème and Lohengrin (the most severe
Wagner acceptable south of Naples
then). There he used to sit, a Greek,
one of a few tenthousand Greeks,
who did not notice half a million Egyptians.
Lived in a Europe of the mind
stuck in the age of Strabo: 'the most grandiose
emporium of the inhabited world,'
which now consists of stone and sea
and a feeling of utter exhaustion.

Rosmarie Waldrop

Zerstoben in heißem Dampf

Steinchen fallen in die Schritte
am Atheneion vorbei, am Café Pastroudis,
vorbei auf aufgerissenen Trottoirs
an den Resten des Hammam,
der einst sechs Monate lang mit Büchern
beheizt wurde, auf Weisung des Kalifen,
wie 4000 andere öffentliche Bäder in Alexandria.
Sechs ganze Monate dauerte es,
nach Augenzeugenberichten, dann waren
alle Schriftrollen der Großen Bibliothek verbrannt.
Armes Land! Vom dynastischen Durcheinander
noch ganz benommen, die Luft glühende Wolle,
die Brüste der Ammen schwarz, ging der Versuch,
alles Wissen vollständig zu horten,
,der Versuch', in den Worten eines alten Rhetoren,
,die Grenzen der Welt zu überwinden',
in Funken auf, in heißen Dampf
um die fettgrauen Leiber der Eroberer –
,in Dampf zerstoben', wenn es das gibt,
aber gab es nicht alles auf der Rue Rosette,
der alten Kanopischen Straße,
die jetzt Sharia Horreya heißt?
Wieder sind die Feigen-Caterer auf ihr unterwegs,
mit schnellen Schritten,
Steinchen fallen in ihre Rufe
und tönen sie zu Lügen, von der Corniche geschönt,
ein ewiges Tosen vielleicht
auf das Bestehen der Welt.

from *Keiner gefriert anders*

Gone up in hot steam

Pebbles fall into your paces
past the Atheneion, past Café Pastroudis,
walking the torn-up pavements
past what remains of the hamam,
which once was heated six months long
with books, on the Caliph's orders,
along with 4,000 other public baths in Alexandria.
Six whole months it took, eye-witnesses reported;
at the end of that time, every last one of the scrolls
in the Great Library had gone up in flames.
Poor country! Still stunned to the core
by dynastic upheavals, the air scorching wool,
the breasts of the wet-nurses black,
the attempt to hoard the entirety of knowledge,
'the attempt', in the words of a rhetor of old,
'to pass beyond the bounds of the very world',
gone up in sparks, in hot steam enfolding
the fatty-grey bodies of the conqueror race –
'gone up in a spray of steam', if that is possible,
but was not everything possible in the rue Rosette,
the old Canopian Road
now known as Sharia Horreya?
The vendors of figs are out and about once again,
walking the streets at a rapid pace,
pebbles falling into their cries
and shading them to lies whitened by the corniche,
perhaps a never-ending uproar
in celebration of the world's endurance.

Michael Hulse

from *No one freezes differently*

Alexandrie, Boulevard de Ramleh, 1903

Wie die Bleistiftschrift auf der alten Postkarte
déposé No 10 erklärt, ist Ramleh der Name eines Badeorts,
einer Hauptstraße im Ausländerviertel der Stadt
und eines Bahnhofs mit Zügen an die Küste.
Auf der Karte macht der Boulevard im rötlichen Staub
einen leichten Schwung auf den Bahnhof zu,
als müsse es jederzeit die Möglichkeit geben,
der sommerlichen Erstarrung zu entfliehen
Richtung Meer, Richtung Ramleh, Richtung Athen.
Die ganze verrottete Langeweile dieses Viertels,
wie sie sich Carlo Mieli, Fabrikant der kolorierten Karte,
nicht dachte, ist gegenwärtig:
eine Apathie ohne Geruch
wie eine Rose aus gewachster Seide.
Wo bleibt der Orient? Herr Mieli hat Sorge getragen.
Rechts neben die Wohnhäuser der Ausländer,
ihre weißen Markisen und Balkons,
und die Figurinen auf der Straße, zu klein,
um wirklich ausdruckslos zu sein,
ließ er eine Rotunde ein.
In diesem Kreis sieht man die Nubierin, verschleiert,
den Mann mit Fez und den promisken Knaben.
Sie posieren unter zerfransten Bananenblättern
mit fortan unbewegtem Gesicht,
unter der Lupe aufgelöst in braune Punkte,
die alles sein können, das heißt nichts,
oder nur die versprühte Wärme dieser Körper
von der Farbe und Härte der Olive.
Doch der Blick geht immer zurück
auf diesen öden Boulevard, zu einem Strichmännchen,
europäisch gekleidet, das vor dem Bahnhof
in eine dunkle Gasse biegt zu guter Letzt,
Kavafis vielleicht, damals 40 Jahre alt,
obwohl alles dagegen spricht und alles
für die Entdeckung der Nähe des Meeres.

from *Keiner gefriert anders*

Alexandrie: Boulevard de Ramleh, 1903

As the pencil script on the old postcard
déposé No. 10 declares: Ramleh is a beach resort,
a main street in the foreigners' district,
and a station for trains to the coast.
The boulevard on the card makes in the reddish dust
a slight curve on the way to the station,
as if it always had to be possible
to escape from summer's fixity and travel
toward the sea, toward Ramleh, toward Athens.
The entire lethargic decrepitude of this district
such as Carlo Mieli, maker of the coloured card,
never thought of, is apparent:
an odourless apathy,
like a rose of waxed silk.
Where did the Orient go? Signor Mieli saw to that.
To the right, beside the foreigners' houses,
their white awnings and balconies,
and the figurines on the street, too small
to be actually expressionless,
he admitted a rotunda.
In this orbit one sees, veiled, the Nubian woman,
the man in a fez, the depraved boy.
With hereafter motionless faces
they pose beneath tattered banana leaves,
and under magnification melt into brown spots
which can be everything, that's to say, nothing,
or merely the vaporized warmth of these bodies
with the hue and hardness of an olive about them.
Yet one's gaze keeps on going back,
over this empty boulevard, to a matchstick man,
in European attire, who turns at long last
into a dark alley facing the station,
Cavafy perhaps, forty years old at the time,
though everything speaks against it, everything
speaks for discovering that the sea is near.

Christopher Middleton

Haken & Augen

Im Meer auf vier gläsernen Krebsen
stand der Pharos, ein Wunder der Welt.
Ganz aus Glas waren die Tiere, 20 Fuß tief im Wasser,
und so groß, daß ein Mann, selbst ausgestreckt,
eine Schere nicht umfassen konnte, berichten
übereinstimmend viele. Es mag daher stimmen.

                     Vom Leuchtturm
ist nichts auf uns gekommen, vom Glas der Panzer
schimmert noch heute die See. Wir glauben daran,
diesem Schimmer zuliebe, und daß der Hafen
als Zone extravaganten Bauens ausgewiesen war.
Pläne für eine neue Bibliothek belegen es, großmütige,
mit Türmen aus Eisen und Kupfer unterm Meeresspiegel
und einem Schacht bis nach Zypern. Der Krieg dann
mit Pergamon über Papyrus und Bücher kam teuer
und vereitelte vieles.

                  Viele Hirngespinste. Viele Lieben.
Sie gingen wie Augen aus, schrieb der sentimentalische Freund
des Dichters. Ein Landgang auf kallaweißem Fickbett
(‚und versprich mir zu sagen, wenn es kommt')
endete in Scherben, in schwarzen Bremsspuren
am Kai. Und nirgends ein Hinweis,
was die Lippen und die Haut erinnerten, außer
in seinen Versen, die mit sich selbst beschäftigt bleiben,
und aufgeregt, zu dieser Zeit der Nacht.

from *Keiner gefriert anders*

Hooks and eyes

In the sea, on four glass crabs,
stood the Pharos, a wonder of the world.
The animals were entirely glass, twenty feet deep in the water,
and so large a man, even stretched out,
could not reach around one claw, many
reports agree. So it might be true.

                Of the lighthouse
nothing has come down to us; the sea still shimmers today
with the glass of the crabs. We believe in them
for the sake of this shimmer, and believe that the harbor
was accounted a zone of extravagant construction.
Plans for a new library prove it, lavish,
with towers of iron and copper under the surface of the sea
and a tunnel all the way to Cyprus. Then the war
with Pergamon over papyrus and books was costly
and thwarted many things.

                Many fancies. Many loves.
They went out like eyes, wrote the sentimental friend
of the poet. A shore leave fucking on a calla-white bed
('and promise you'll say when it comes')
ended in pieces, in black skid marks
on the quay. And nowhere a clue
to what the lips and the skin remembered, except
in his verses, which remain concerned with themselves,
and nervous, at this time of night.

Andrew Shields

Das Zimmer über dem Café

Krevettenfarben
unter dem blauen Hemd
stellt er ihn sich vor.
Sommer. Sommer
sein Name.
Wird er kommen?
Kommt er?
Helle ist mit einem Mal
in der Tür, Stimmen vom Café.
Schabenbraun ist der Sommer,
braun das Bettgestell.

Sie verstecken den Lärm
unter der Zunge.
Sicherheit des Schwankens
im Licht dieses Zimmers.
Wenn sie Nähe gefunden haben,
hören sie nicht auf.
Sie halten die Nähe an.

from *Keiner gefriert anders*

The room above the café

Prawn-coloured
he imagines him
beneath his blue shirt.
Summer. Summer is
his name.
Will he come?
Is he coming now?
Brightness is all at once
at the door, voices from the café.
The summer is cockroach-brown,
brown the bedstead.

They hide the din
beneath their tongues.
Secure as they sway
in the light of this room.
When they've come close
they don't let up.
They catch their closeness.

Richard Dove

Kavafis widerspricht Seneca

Du bist wie eine Blume, sagte er auf deutsch.
Er sagte es jedem. Er wollte nicht glauben,
daß Alexandria eines dieser Bordelle sei,
von den Göttern geschenkt, in denen wir
schrankenlos frei waren. Zu Hause, in der Lepsius 7,
machte er kein Licht, um besser
mit den *verbotenen* Erinnerungen und Bildern
spielen zu können. Zwischen den Seiten alter Bücher
suchte er nach deinen Wimpern. Zuweilen
sagte er zu dir oder zu einem anderen Gast:
Ich habe Lust, in das Schlafzimmer zu gehen.
Dieser Akzent, leichter von Jalousie
zu Jalousie! Er hob
den erstickenden Baldachin
mit weißen, schlaffen, schönen Armen.
Schau, was sie mit mir gemacht haben,
schien er zu sagen, was sie auf mich
geschrieben haben. Nimm es!

Cavafy contradicts Seneca

You're like a flower, he said in Heine's German.
He said it to everyone. Couldn't believe
that Alexandria's one of those brothels
gifted by the gods, in which we were
boundlessly free. At home at 7 Lepsius Street,
he didn't light the lamps so as to be able
to play all the better with *forbidden*
memories, images. Searched between the pages of old books
for your eyelashes. On occasion,
he'd say to you or another guest:
'I feel a desire to repair to the bedroom.'
This accent, lighter from blind
to blind! He lifted
the stifling baldacchino
with white, lethargic, handsome arms.
Look what they have done to me,
he seemed to be saying, what they have
written on me. Take it!

Richard Dove

Wer aus mir trinkt

Die eine Ägypterin
ließ sie sich nie von einem Griechen küssen.
Es hätte sie um den Mund gebracht.
Doch Verse schrieb sie.
Verse zerriß sie, die alte Kältin.
Ihr Haar ließ sie wachsen
für deine weißen Füße.
Ich bin nichts als das, sagte sie, Brüste,
Feige, Locken. Datteläugig.
Früher (es war einmal) geschah,
wenn sie sich zeigte, Stille.
Sie hielt mit ihrem Atem Schrift,
Schritt mit den Schabstellen
im Innern der Schenkel, aus schwarzen Ovalen
gezupft. Ah, die Schwerkraft der Regenschnüre!
Sie ruht. Dieser Vers ist ein Schatten der Liebe.

from *Keiner gefriert anders*

Whoever drinks from me

That one Egyptian woman
did not accept a Grecian kiss.
She said it would have filched away her mouth.
However, she wrote verses.
She rent the verses, that ancient Coldian.
She grew her hair
for your white feet.
I am nothing but this, she said, breast,
fig, locks. For eyes, dates.
Before (in a time long ago) when she revealed herself
silence came to pass.
She kept score with her breath,
a scoring on the inside of her thigh – those black ovals
twitched. Alas, the gravity of the cords of rain!
She rests. This verse is the shadow of love.

Robert Gray

Litanei

Er steigt in Sarwat ein. Nach San Stefano,
Zizinia, Mazloum, Glymenopoulo, Sidi Gaber,
Cleopatra, Sporting, Ibrahimieh, Camp de César,
Chatby, Mazarita steigt er in Ramleh aus.
Er hat Nüsse gegessen und aus der Ferne,
die jetzt näher ist, das Meer gesehen. Jetzt
ist er bei der Villa des Ludovico Salvatore, der
hier die ,Winterträumereien in meinem Garten
in Ramleh' schrieb (1914 als Privatdruck in Prag
erschienen). Mit Mühe lauscht er den Stimmen,
die je nach der Baumart so verschieden sind.
In ihrem *Laubgepolter* sagt er sich, *wie ein Springen*
in Sätzen, die Namen aller Haltestellen nochmals auf.

from *Keiner gefriert anders*

Litany

He gets on at Sarwat. After San Stefano,
Zizinia, Mazloum, Glymenopoulo, Sidi Gaber,
Cleopatra, Sporting, Ibrahimieh, Camp de César,
Chatby, Mazarita he alights in Ramleh.
He's eaten nuts and from the distance,
although closer now, he's seen the ocean. Now
he's near the villa of Ludovico Salvatore, who wrote
'Winter Reveries in my Garden
in Ramleh' (privately printed in Prague
in 1914) here. With difficulty he attends to the voices
which are so different depending on the type of tree.
Within their *leaf-rumbling* he recites to himself *like the leaping
in sentences* the names of all the stops, over again.

Robert Gray

Alexandria (2)

Nicht in den Augen, an den Kiemen
siehst du, ob der Barsch heute nacht
gefangen wurde, belehren die *mazmazelles*
auf dem Fischmarkt in der Rue Memphis.
Er schlendert unter Segeltuch,
lauscht dem Gerede, dem Klingeln langer Löffel
in hohen Limonadengläsern. ,Ägypten hat die längsten Stunden
der Welt', erinnert er sich, und an einen anderen Satz
seiner Mutter: ,Warum von jemandem verlangen,
daß er jemanden auf die gleiche Weise liebt?'
Es war Nacht gewesen, und er war heimlich,
vermummt in Hut und Schal, aus dem Atterine-Viertel
heimgekehrt. Sie sprachen auf dem Balkon,
unter zyperngelbem Gestirn, und erinnernd
(sich erinnernd, daß der junge griechische Arbeiter
unter den Achseln nach Joghurt roch) fühlt er sich
plötzlich rein und aufgelöst. Rein wie
in Reinigung oder darein sich fügen,
wie in Zeugenschaft.

from *Keiner gefriert anders*

Alexandria (2)

Not from the eyes, from the gills
you can tell if the perch was caught
tonight, instruct the *mazmazelles*
at the fish market in rue Memphis.
He strolls beneath the sail-cloth,
listening carefully to the tittle-tattle, the clanking of tall spoons
in lemonade-glasses. 'Egypt has the longest hours
in the world', he reminds himself; and another of his mother's
sayings: 'Why demand someone
love another in the selfsame way?'
It had been night and he had secretly
returned, masked in hat and scarf,
from the Atterine quarter. They talked on the balcony
beneath the Cyprus-yellow constellations, reminiscing
(about the young Greek worker's armpits
that smelt of yogurt) and suddenly
he felt pure and shriven. Pure as
in purification, and as in the pure submission
of procreation.

Robert Gray

Bericht von Rika

Einmal, als wir mit dem kleinen Koffer kamen,
berichtet Rika Singolopoulos, weinte er. Er nahm
den Block und schrieb darauf: ‚Diesen Koffer
kaufte ich vor 30 Jahren, in Hast, für eine Reise
nach Kairo, um mich zu vergnügen. Damals
war ich jung und schön, und nicht häßlich.'
In den Koffer legte er den alten Morgenmantel,
den mit den roten Litzen, und die Sammlung
Gedichte auf losen Blättern.
Er wollte den Patriarchen nicht sehen,
als dieser ins Hospital kam, unangemeldet,
und dann empfing er ihn doch und erhielt,
es ist nicht festgehalten, die Sakramente.
Nicht Materialist genug hatte der Alexandriner
ein Gran Furcht vor dem Unbekannten.
Sein Grab fand ich nicht.

from *Keiner gefriert anders*

Rika's report

Once, when we came with that little case,
reported Rika Singolopoulos, he wept. Took up
the writing-pad, wrote on it: 'I bought
this case thirty years ago, hastily, for a trip
to Cairo to have a good time. Back then,
I was young and good-looking, not hideous.'
He put his old dressing-gown into the case,
the one with the red braid, and the
loose-leaf collection of poems.
He didn't want to see the patriarch
when this man of God came unannounced to the hospital
but then changed his mind and received
(there's no record) the sacraments.
Not materialistic enough, this Alexandrian
felt a modicum of fear of the unknown.
I couldn't locate his grave.

Richard Dove

Was übrig blieb

Im griechischen Konsulat, unter dem Dach,
den Balken, die in der Hitze sieden
und reißen,
stehen Reste: zwei Sessel, das dunkle Holz
der Armlehnen an den Griffen weiß von Schweiß,
ein Spiegel, osmanisch, mit Intarsien und Ösen,
an denen seltsame Messinggefäße hängen,
zum Verbrennen von Weihrauch einst? Alles
ist schwer, staubbeladen, die Waschkrüge
bemalt mit *rosae hibernicae,* die Bibliothek
zerfleddert und beraubt.
Es läßt sich nichts zusammenreimen.
Falls es einen Besitzer dieser Reste gab,
dann ist er nirgends oder geflohen über das Meer
oder in die andere Richtung über die Salzseen
oder er ist hinter diesen Spiegel gepreßt,
mit seinem Schatten, seinen wohlerzogenen Manieren,
dem alten Schal, in dem er sich verbarg,
wenn er aufbrach in die Rue d'Anastasi.
Unlesbar sind die Reste geworden
wie das Wasser über den Steinen.
So wie Glanz mit Glanz erlischt.

from *Keiner gefriert anders*

What was left

At the Greek Consulate, under the roof,
the crossbeams that sizzle in the heat
and crack, stand
remnants: two armchairs, the dark wood
at the handrests bleached by sweat,
a mirror, Ottoman, with marquetry and lugs
for hanging curious metal vessels –
in which to burn incense? Everything
is ponderous, thick with dust, the wash basins
painted with *rosae hibernicae,* the library
tattered and pillaged.
A hodge-podge here, nothing to make sense.
If anyone ever owned these remnants,
he's nowhere, or fled across the ocean,
or over the salt-lakes in the opposite direction,
or in behind the mirror he is pressed
with his shadow, his civilized manners,
the old shawl in which he hid
whenever he set out for the Rue d'Anastasi.
The remnants have become illegible,
like water crossing stones.
As one radiance extinguishes another.

Christopher Middleton

Alexandria (3)

für Adonis

Ein öder Betonstrich.
Hier wächst du nicht an.
Nichts als junge Matrosen am Hafen,
in schwarzer Uniform, die lebendige
silbrige Masse der Fische in Kisten,
und Mädchen, die alle, so sagt man,
die Gabe des Tanzes haben,
des Schwimmens und des Liebens.

Breccia ließ unter dem Billard Palace graben.
So tief liegt die römische Stadt wie die Zimmer
hoch sind im ersten Stock.
Alle diese Toten um uns herum.
Wo sie beerdigen wenn nicht
in der Sprache? Und weiter draußen
die Wüste, Steine, Sterne, Nacht, Nichts.

Das Meer klagt, vom Wahn besessen,
von einer einzigen Welle sterben zu können.
Hier schlägst du nicht an.

from *Keiner gefriert anders*

Alexandria (3)

for Adonis

A desolate expanse of concrete.
You can't grow on this.
Nothing but young sailors in the port,
in black uniforms, the living
silvery mass of fish in crates,
and girls who all, they say,
are grand mistresses of dancing,
of swimming, and of loving.

Breccia had them dig under the Billard Palace.
The Roman city lies as deep below
as the first floor rooms are high.
All of these dead about us.
Where to inter them, if not
in language? And, farther out,
the desert, stones, stars, night, nothingness.

The sea laments, possessed by a mad hope
that it might die of a single wave.
You can't break on this.

Michael Hulse

Konstantin K.

Sterne wie die weiß gekochten Augen der Fische.
Hier in die Nacht legte er seinen Weg.
Seine von Durst benommenen Worte rieselten
den fort und fort währenden Abschieden hinterher.

Schon richtig: Diese Salbe gibt (arabische Illusion!)
der Haut die Farbe des Mondes. Und rot
bleibt, mit Haarspray bewahrt, die Rose.
Wir sind unzerbrechlich, wollen wir glauben,

gezeichnet von den späten Hieben des Glücks.
Sie lagen bei ihm, längliche Liturgie der Glieder,
als gingen sie nie, und spät erst begann er,
die erinnerte Lust zu verhütten. Er wußte:

Die Stadt mißt nicht die Zeit. Sie bildet sie ab.
Ihr Wissen bröselt über Generationen hinab
in Gräber. Liebe gibt es ,die Hitze eines Blicks'.
Doch wiegt Reinheit ohnehin gering für den Nil.

Constantine C.

Stars like fish eyes boiled white.
Here in the night he made his way.
Dazed by thirst, his words drizzled along
behind the ever ongoing farewells.

It's true: this ointment gives the skin
(Arabian illusion!) the color of the moon. And red,
preserved with hairspray, remains the rose.
We'd like to believe we're indestructible,

marked by the late blows of fortune. They lay
beside him, an elongated liturgy of limbs,
as if they'd never leave, and only later did he begin
to smelt the desire he recalled. He knew:

the city doesn't measure time. It reproduces it.
Its knowledge crumbles down the generations
into graves. There's love 'the heat of a gaze.'
But anyway, purity weighs little for the Nile.

Andrew Shields

Drei unveröffentlichte Gedichte aus dem Nachlaß
von Konstantin Kavafis

Der Kai

Man brachte sie in die hohlen Schiffe zurück.
Im Sand blieb der Abdruck ihrer Körper,
Fleck von Haaren, Blut.
Im Sand blieben die Körper der Feinde, die Sieger
waren, atmeten sie noch.
Die Medien berichteten drei Tage darüber.
Die Schiffe wurden Flugzeuge, Speere Minen,
es gab mehr Vergewaltigungen als Männer.
Dann ging man zur Tagesordnung über.
Die Schiffe fuhren, tief im Wasser, heim.

So las er die Nachbilder einer verheerenden Welt.
So suchte er, nicht unschuldig, die Vergangenheit.
Er schätzte die Schreiber,
bei denen es kein Vergessen gab.
Nur dort hatte das Gedächtnis einen Ort,
außer den Gräbern,
und er gehörte ihm und jedem allein.

from *Keiner gefriert anders*

Three unpublished poems from the estate of Constantine Cavafy

The quay

Then they brought them back to the hollow ships.
The imprints of their bodies were left behind in the sand,
with bits of hair, blood.
In the sand were left behind the corpses of their foes, who would
have been victors if they'd still had breath.
The media gave it coverage for three days.
The ships became aircraft, the spears became mines,
there were more cases of rape than men.
Then it was business as usual.
The ships sailed home, sagging deep in the water.

Thus he scanned the after-images of a world's devastation.
Thus he trawled, no innocent, the past.
He valued those writers
in whom there is no appetite for oblivion.
Only in them could memory find a location
apart from in graves,
and that site belonged to him and to everyone, alone.

Robert Gray

Auf dem Spiegel

Zum Vergangenen zurückkehren und es anschauen:
den unauslöschlichen Rückzug des Gerölls am Ende des Hafens,
eilige Wolken, ein Fruchtschiff aus Haifa,
schnittig, innen kühl. Später den Mond,
der im Hof den Winter aufsagt.

Wie ein Bild auf dem Spiegel
dringt mein Schmerz nicht in ihn ein.
Jetzt erst, ohne ihn, erinnre ich
die genossenen Freuden. Die kleine Lampe
am Bett war der einzige Zeuge

der Verklammerung und
des Rückzugs. Der Hafen, das Geröll,
Knochenstücke an Mund und Rücken,
die Münze unter den Kieseln,
die blinkende Stimme:
‚Bist du schon lange hier?'

from *Keiner gefriert anders*

On the mirror

To go back to the past and look at it:
the inexpungible retreat of shingle where the harbour ends,
clouds hurrying, a fruit-ship out of Haifa,
streamlined, cool inside. Later the moon
reciting in the courtyard winter's arrival.

Like an image on the mirror
my pain does not penetrate it.
Only now, without it, do I recall
the pleasures experienced. The little lamp
beside the bed a single witness

to the intertwining and
to the retreat. The harbour, the shingle,
pieces of bone at the mouth and back,
the coin beneath the pebbles,
the voice a flash:
'Have you been here long?'

Christopher Middleton

from *No one freezes differently*

Poetik

von Konstantin Kavafis verworfenes Gedicht, geschrieben vor dem Jüngling
von Motya, Marmor, 180 cm, 460–450 v. Chr.

Das Gedicht
sucht einen Ort
für die Schachzüge meines Verlangens.
Es kann es nicht offen tun.
Erspart mir Erklärungen.
Die Stadt ist eine Bürde.

Fabel, Apokryphe: Alter Stoff
verhüllt die Schenkel,
das gelbe Mal an der Leiste
mit dem Flaum.
Helles Gesirr, bedenk ich's,
über der Haut wie von
Einenachtlibellen.

Es ist Gaze, gesponnen
aus steinernem weißesten Stein.
Aus vielfach gebrochenem Flügel.
Widrig breche ich

wieder den alten Stoff
mit Sprache: Worten,
die ich vor der Bourse, im Café,
im teerfarbnen Zimmer
hörte. Auflas in alten
Geschichtsbüchern. Das Gedicht
mag keine Verzierung. Es ist
auf Stilisierung aus: Plissé,
das die Stärke
der Wölbung verrät.

Ein Gedicht ist für niemanden.
Ich schicke es meinen Freunden,
die Freiheit, es zu verstehen
oder nicht zu verstehen.

from *Keiner gefriert anders*

Poetics

poem rejected by Constantine Cavafy, written in front of the youth of Motya, marble, 180 cm, 460–450 BC

The poem
seeks a place
for the chess moves of my desire.
It cannot do it openly.
Spare me explanations.
The city is a burden.

Fable, apocrypha: old material
hides the thighs,
the yellow spot on the groin
with the down.
High buzzing, if I think on it,
over the skin like that of
one-night dragonflies.

It is gauze, spun
from stony whitest stone.
From a multiply broken wing.
Against my will, I break

again the old material
with language: words
I heard in front of the bourse,
in the café, in the tar-colored
room. Picked up in old
history books. The poem
does not like decoration. It is
after stylization: plissé
betraying the curve's
strength.

A poem is for nobody.
I send it to my friends,
the freedom to understand it
or not to understand.

from *No one freezes differently*

Auf seinem Weg hat es
Splitter des Nichts gesammelt,
um blendend
dazustehen am Ende.

from *Keiner gefriert anders*

On its way it has
gathered splinters of nothing,
to stand there
splendid at the end.

Andrew Shields

from
Ich habe die Nacht
Mine is the night
(2003)

Auf dem Weg zum Grabmal des Kleoboulos

Seine Gedichte aber, die er verfaßte, sind an der Zahl über dreitausend Verse.
Ein kurzer Brief an Solon ist noch vorhanden.
A. Heinold, *Biographien aller bekannten griechischen und lateinischen*
Autoren, Wien, Prag, 1800

Jetzt leeren sich die Augen vom Licht des Sommers.
Jetzt leert sich das Meer.
Jetzt erfüllt sich Sprache im Zuhören.
Was hat sie gemacht das Jahr über?
Was hast du gesucht über die Jahre?

Der Weg, kaum Weg, geht durch steinige Felder.
Wir werden größer, weil das Licht sanfter wird,
versuchen Gleichgewicht zu halten,
als stünden wir auf einem Rad oder einer Kugel
wie jene nackte schwere Frau auf alten Bildern.
Die Kugel rollt. Welt tut sich auf.
Das Grabmal wächst und lebt gegen diese Welt,
neue Buchten, Berge im Abenddunst.
Auf einen Baum kommen eine Million Steine.
Wir müssen nur hinhören.
Sie sind die Lungen eines alten Gotts.

Von einem Felsen blicken wir ins Meer.
Die Lichtreflexe auf seiner blauen Haut
sind ein Knäuel Sterne, und
selten, an den Sternen vorbei,
schauen wir in der Tiefe des Wassers
den Grund aus Stein und Sand von Steinen.

So gehen wir weiter, zwischen Oberfläche und Tiefe,
zwischen Steinen und geriffeltem Sand,
eingebunden in das Bündel eignen Lebens.
Hatte wir Zeit zu sehen, zu hören, zu lieben?
Wir gehen zum Grabmal, nirgendwohin sehr schnell.
Aus Furcht, ohne Mond den Weg zurück
nicht zu finden, und weil wir ohne Eis kalt
uns nicht bescheiden, nicht glauben wollen,
daß alles auf der Erde durchwühlt ist,
aller Wortraum, Weltraum, weißes Meer,

from *Ich habe die Nacht*

On the way to the tomb of Kleoboulos

The poems he wrote, however, numbered more than three thousand verses.
A brief letter to Solon has survived.
A. Heinold, *Biographien aller bekannten griechischen und lateinischen*
Autoren. Wien-Prag, 1800

Now the eyes are being emptied of summer light.
Now the sea is being emptied.
Now language brims, being listened to.
What has she been doing for the past year?
What were you looking for, over the years?

The way, barely a way, goes through stony fields.
We grow bigger, because the light is softer,
and as if we stood on a wheel or a sphere
like that weighty naked woman in the old pictures,
we try to keep our balance.
The sphere rolls. World opens up.
The tomb grows and lives counter to this world,
the new bays, mountains in the evening mist.
A million stones amount to one tree.
We have only to be listening.
Of an old god they are the lungs.

From a clifftop we look into the sea.
The lights reflected on its blue skin
are a cluster of stars, and
seldom do we see, past the stars,
in the depth of the water,
the floor of stone and sand from stones.

So we walk on, between surface and depth,
between stones and rippled sand, each of us
wrapped into the bundle of his own life.
Did we have time to see, to hear, to love?
We go to the tomb, nowhere very fast.
In fear that, moonless, we might not find
the way back, and because, chill, without ice,
we are reluctant to acquiesce, to believe
that everything on earth has been rummaged through,
that the entire word-space, world-space, the white sea,

from *Mine is the night*

die Szene kleiner, Lindos eine Vorstadt
von Hongkong, Alexandria ein Abfall
von New York, Edda in Accra.
Die globalen Spiele sind ferner als der Sand
in der Tiefe. Im Gebüsch ist die Altmutter
bei den Ziegen. Das Feigenblatt braun und nah.

Der Herbst: ein Bild. Jenes des eignen Lebens,
das wir nie vergessen konnten. Du warst da,
mehr bei den Fingern als bei den Versen.
Ich kenne deine Finger. Meisterin der Hände.
Du berührtest mich wie mit nassen Zweigen.
Ich rieb den Dorn am Haar vorbei, ich kannte
den Ton, meine Geliebte, den Tau auf dir.
Meiner letzten, meiner ersten Geliebten.

Auf den Hügeln verstreut liegen die Steine
wie Winterfrüchte auf breiten Borden,
nicht vom Wind bewegt. Von der Hitze
gespalten, von einem Beben verdrückt.
Von keiner monarchischen Macht.
Angeblich hat der Orient Rhodos beeinflußt.
Im fernen Athen vermaß Philoktet hundert junge Männer,
um das rechte Maß zu finden, jenen Durchschnitt,
der erhaben und göttlich ist.
Was ist dem Menschen zuzumuten?
Alles in Maßen, sagte Kleoboulos
in seinem kurzen Brief an Solon.
Sein Rundgrab, aus schwarzen Quadern,
widerspricht der Landschaft, wächst aus ihr
und weist sie ab. Behaupten wir uns so
gegen Zumutung? Tragen und treiben wir?

Was hast du gesucht über das Jahr?
Hätte deine Zunge Glanz, wären
deine Finger zu mir gesprungen,
hätten die Steine die Luft geteilt,
wärst du hier, Meisterin der Hände.

Dieser Ort ist angenehm,
wärst du hier. Cafés an jeder Ecke,
verschwiegene Einlässe, Taxis,
die auf dich warten, wenn es regnet,

from *Ich habe die Nacht*

the spectacle is smaller, Lindos a suburb
of Hong Kong, Alexandria detritus
of New York, Edda in Accra.
The global games are more remote than the sand
at a depth. Among bushes, with goats,
the ancestress. Figleaf, near, and brown.

Autumn: an image. Image of one's own life,
never to be forgotten. You were there,
more with fingers than with lines of verse.
I know your fingers. Mistress of hands.
As if with wet twigs you touched me.
Thorns tugged my hair as I brushed by, I knew
the sound, beloved mine, the dew upon you.
You my last, my first belovèd.

On the hills the stones lie scattered
like winter fruits on wide boards,
not moved by wind. Split
by heat, dispersed by a trembling.
By no monarchical power.
Supposedly the Orient influenced Rhodes.
In far-off Athens, Philoktetes took the measure
of a hundred young men, to find the average,
that right measure, sublime, godlike.
What demands are laid on people?
All in due measure, said Kleoboulos
in his brief letter to Solon.
His round tomb of black squared stones
contradicts the landscape, grows out of it
and waves it away. Against the demands
do we also persist? Do we bear fruit, and flourish?

This year past, what were you looking for?
If your tongue had a shine, your fingers,
had they leaped at me, had
the stones portioned out the air,
then, mistress of hands, here is where you'd be.

This place is pleasant,
if you were here. Cafés at every corner,
hushed openings, taxis
which wait for you when rain is falling,

wenn der Regen das Amphitheater
in ein kleines Meer verwandelt, ohne Sicht auf Schiffe.
Was hast du gesucht, als unsere Liebe verdorrte?
Was hast du gesucht, in Geschäften gehalten,
in Städten, die schneller noch sich verändern
als dein Herz, in Büchern, zwischen Steinen,
die Schatten jetzt zu leichter Asche macht?

In dem weiten Haus war alles da,
Stühle, Tisch, Geschirr, Nägel,
,pietre dure', zusammengeführt zu einer Ordnung,
die von dir kam und die du jetzt nicht mehr klar erkennst,
nur noch in den abgefallenen Blättern vor dem Haus.
Wie sagte Kleoboulos?
,Lest in den abgefallenen Blättern'?

Am Strand waren die Sucher des Papiers unterwegs.
Jetzt treten alle ab. Bevor das Licht schwindet,
geht noch ein Strahl durch die Landschaft.
Ein Strahl, waagrecht über den hufgefurchten Pfaden.
Er trocknet die Formen aus.

Jetzt ist es dunkel.
Der Docht schon unterm Horizont.
Dünner Rauch, der sich kräuselt.
Erinnerungen, Silben und Vornamen,
verdunsten wie Körperwärme.
Wir sind erregt. Ein Bedürfnis
läßt nicht nach: Die Vergangenheit
zurückzuholen oder eine Zukunft
uns vorzustellen. Der Tod wär umsonst.

Immer sind wir allein mit der Sprache, zugerichtet von ihr.
Eingebunden in unser Bündel Worte strengen wir sie an,
Vergangenheit zu nennen. Was hat sie gemacht über das Jahr?
Sie hat Widerstand geleistet. Sie nahm wenig von uns auf.
So wie wir unsere Haut dem Licht, der Sonne gaben,
so reichten wir ihr, der gegebensten, unsere Erfahrung.
Aber sie schwebte. Zählte nicht die Blätter, die fielen.
Dunkelte nicht ab. Mag sie das Herz härten,
an die Stille vor den Worten, ans erste Geräusch
der Welt, das Pfeifen der Atome,
den Tinitus im Herzen hält sie sich nicht.

from *Ich habe die Nacht*

when rain converts the amphitheatre
into a small ocean, with no ship in sight.
What were you looking for when our love dried up?
What looking for, detained by business
in cities that change more rapidly still
than your heart, in books, among stones
which shadows turn into light ash?

In the spacious house, everything was there,
chairs, a table, silverware, nails,
pietre dure, assembled into an order
which came from you and which you no longer clearly
acknowledge – except in fallen leaves at the door.
What did Kleoboulos say?
Was it 'Read among the fallen leaves'?

They patrolled the shore, the searchers for paper.
Now they've quit. Before the light goes,
one more ray penetrates the landscape.
A ray, transverse over the tracks furrowed
by hoofs. It desiccates the forms.

Now it is dark.
The wick already below the horizon.
Thin smoke curling in upon itself.
Memories, mere syllables and first names,
dissipate like body-heat.
We are excited. One need
never desists. To bring back the past,
or to imagine a future. Death would be for nothing.

Always we're alone with language, beset by her.
Strung into our bundle of words we exert her
to name the past. All year long, what did she do?
She was resisting. She took scant notice of us.
As we gave our skin to the light, to the sun,
to her, the givenmost, we handed our experience.
But she was floating, counted no falling leaves,
did not darken. Harden her heart as she may,
on the silence preceding the words, on the first
noise of the world, the whistling of atoms,
the tinnitus in the heart, she does not dwell.

Sie wartet auf die Ankunft der Bilder.
Sie gleicht der Geliebten, die mit dir
die Liebe entdecken will. Die bereit ist,
alles zu denken, was du mit ihr denken möchtest.
Die Sprache, die Geriebene, am Mund Wunde.

Alles ein Schatten, sagte Kleoboulos.
(Ein Zeugnis dafür gibt es nicht.)

Jetzt ist es Nacht, nachtfinster.
Jetzt ist dem Blick das schwarze rollende Land
entzogen. Nicht dem Wort, seiner Kraft.
Nicht der Geliebten, ihren Handreichungen.
Das Rundgrab des Kleoboulos ist eine Sternwarte.
Der Mond kommt nicht. So vieles hat sie
nicht zu Ende gesprochen. So viel Leidenschaft
in sich versteckt zu finden, hat sie überrascht.
Daß der Mond nicht kommt. Daß sie zur Geschichte
seiner Nichtentdeckung wird. Ein anderer Beginn.
Ein schwarzes Immerglühn. Die Reisen
fangen wieder an. Haben sie aufgehört?
Noch einmal wirft deine Hand Steine unter das Rad.

from *Ich habe die Nacht*

She waits for the images to arrive.
She is like the belovèd who wants with you
to discover love. Who is ready to think
anything you might think with her.
Language, the worn one, the wound at the mouth.

Everything a shadow, said Kleoboulos.
(There's no evidence for this.)

Now it is night, dark as night.
Now the black rolling landscape has withdrawn
from sight. Not from words, their strength.
Not from the belovèd, her outstretching hands.
The round tomb of Kleoboulos is an observatory.
No moon comes. There's so much
she still has to speak of. It surprised her
to find so much passion hidden inside her.
That there is no moon. That she is becoming
the story of its being undiscovered. Another
beginning. A black everglow. The travels
start afresh. Did they ever end?
Your hand once more throws stones beneath the wheel.

Christopher Middleton

from *Mine is the night*   129

Intarsien

Keine Sarkophagwand.
Ein granitenes Schiff
steht glanzlos im Felsen, geschnitzt und grau,
neben der Wegrinne zur Akropolis, hart und grau.
Das Zwischendeck ist ausgebuchtet.
Du kannst Platz nehmen auf dem Granit
und alles zurückverfolgen
bis zum Speer, zu Fackeln und Salben,
dem Samenkleid, das über allem lag.

Es muß gewesen sein
wie vor dem Monitor heute,
neben der stahlummantelten Tonne,
die alles auf einen Klick verstrahlt,
wenn Bibliotheken flache Stollen
in deine Augen treiben
und zig Antworten zwischen Hirn
und lunarer Stirnwand glühen.

Später wird es heißen:
Die Augen, beinerne Intarsien, sind gut erhalten.

from *Ich habe die Nacht*

Inlays

Not a wall of sarcophagi.
A granite ship
stands lustreless in the rock-face, hewn and grey,
beside the runnelled track to the Acropolis, hard and grey.
The 'tween-deck is hollowed out.
You can sit on the granite
and follow it all back
to the spear, the torches and the ointments,
the semen coat that wrapped it all.

It must have been much as it is today
before the monitor,
beside the steel-sheathed box
despatching its rays at a click,
libraries mining your eyes
with their low galleries
and endless answers glowing
between your brain and the lunar wall of your brow.

One day they will say:
the eyes, inlays of bone, are well preserved.

Michael Hulse

Diana

Was hat sie ihm erlaubt zu sehen,
bevor er verwandelt wurde? Den Fuß,
den weißen Knöchel, den Rücken
und die Brust? Was sieht man,
wenn man sieht? Ich habe die Sichel
in ihrem Haar gesehen. Ich habe
den Rücken der Welt im Wasser gesehen,
ich habe das Wasser geschändet, die schnelle,
wahnsinnige Furt. Ich habe das Licht
vom Licht unterschieden.

Danach ist nichts.

Die Bienen schweigen,
die Vögel, die vorbeiziehenden Wolken.
Als schaue die Welt auf meine Rute
im Wasser. Habe ich etwas gesehen?
Mein Fell nimmt den Wind auf,
sträubt sich. Ich rieche den Ort,
wo sie war, wo sie den weißen Fuß
ins Wasser tauchte, ich schabe
der Birke die Haut ab, das Licht.
Meine Hufe versinken im Schlamm.

from *Ich habe die Nacht*

Diana

What did she permit him to see
before he was transformed? Her foot,
her ankle, white, her back
and her breast? What do you see
when you see? I saw the crescent
in her hair. I saw
the back of the world in the water,
I lay with the water – the swift
demented ford. I distinguished the light
from the light.

       But then there is nothing.

       The bees are silent,
the birds, the clouds that are moving past.
As though the world were regarding my pizzle
in the water. Did I see something?
My fur absorbs the wind,
bristles. I can smell the spot
where she was, where she dipped her white foot
into the water, I scrape
the skin – the light – from off the birch-tree.
My hooves are sinking down into the ooze.

Richard Dove

Ayios Kassianos

Vom Fenster Blick auf ein Minarett, das Kreuz heißt
und aus Misr, Ägypten kommt. Nachts hat es
einen Kranz grüner Neonröhren um den dicken Hals.
Nachts riecht übel vom Garten her der Pakistani-Strauch.
Unten, auf der gesperrten Straße, nachts, schimpfen
griechische Soldaten auf türkische, bei den Sandsäcken.
Gesprengte Häuser: angehaltene Zeit. Ohne Jugend ganz.
Die Katzen machen die beiden Lefkosias zu einem Land.

                   Von der Balustrade
fallen verfettete Heuschrecken in ihre spitzen Mäuler.
Sie schärfen und schärfen die Krallen im Sand. Sand-
haufen, Zellhaufen. Nur gut, daß es freundliche Hände
gibt, die dir die Augen schließen, Augen, welche
grundlos bitten, daß die Schale nicht zu hart wird.

(Und wenn du dich streckst, den Granatapfel zu pflücken,
dann mußt du immer wieder kommen in dieses Land,
das bei Famagusta liegt, Lapta, Lefkosia, schwerem Gelb.)

Ayios Kassianos

The window gives onto a minaret by the name of Cross
which comes from Misr, Egypt. At night
it wears a wreath of green neon tubes around its plump neck.
At night the Pakistani bush wafts evil odours across from the
                                                        garden.
Below on the barricaded road, at night, Greek soldiers
curse near the sandbags at Turkish soldiers.
Blasted houses: halted time. No youth far and wide.
The cats make these two Lefkosias into a single land.

                            From the balustrade
dropsical locusts tumble into their whetted mouths.
They sharpen, sharpen their claws in the sand. Clumps
of sand, clumps of cells. Thank goodness for friendly hands
which close your eyes – eyes which beg for no reason
that the shell won't prove too hard.

(And should you stretch to pluck that pomegranate,
you're fated to come back again and again to this tract of land
which lies near Famagusta, Lapta, Lefkosia, heavy yellow.)

Richard Dove

In den ägyptischen Filmen

Turbane jede Menge, und Augen
zu zweit, wie die Mädchen in den Straßen,
von Khôl umschnürt, schwarz, am schwärzesten.
‚Bewahre dir die zwei ewigen Lichter
in der Tiefe deiner schwarzen Augen',
sagt schmachtend der Held. Wir verstehen
nichts, gar nichts, nur daß er sie einlädt
zu den Wegen entlang des Nils, unter die Kühle
der Zweige, und daß eine schöne Frau mehr ist
als ihre langen Brüste, mehr als ihr Garten,
den er gleich bewässert und nicht kann.
‚Ich bin und werde sein, und niemand gibt es,
der mir den Schleier wegreißen könnte.'
So viel Zurückhaltung, feierlich und beklemmend,
erhöht noch durch das alte Zelluloid.
Eine schleiergleiche Ahnung huscht
über Sonnenbrillen, Rückkehr in die Kindheit,
in Kinderspiele vor dem Spiegel, es gebe
nichts Schöneres als dieses Laken, dieses Haar,
dieses epileptische Kindermädchen, das sich
auszieht vor dem stillen Betrachter und
auf ihren Schoß eine rote Katze setzt. Dann
essen wir Datteln und Trauben, strahlend.
Ein Zeremoniell. Diese Filme sind ein Fest.

Vor dem Abspann legt der Held die Lippen
in ihr schwärzestes Haar. Das ist alles.

from *Ich habe die Nacht*

In those Egyptian films

Turbans untold, and eyes
in pairs, like the girls on the streets
laced up with khôl, black, blacker than black.
'Preserve those two eternal lights
in the depths of your black eyes'
says the hero meltingly. We understand
nothing, nothing at all – just that he invites her
to walk the paths along the Nile, beneath the cool
branches, and that a beautiful woman is more
than her long breasts, more than her garden
which he will water at once but can't.
'I am and will be and there is no one
who could tear away my veil.'
So much restraint – dignified, oppressive –
augmented further by the archaic celluloid.
A veil-like suspicion is flitting
across the sunglasses – the return to childhood,
to children's games in front of the mirror – that nothing
can be more lovely than this sheet, this hair,
this epileptic nursemaid undressing
in front of her silenced beholder and placing
a red cat on her lap. We then
eat dates and grapes, in radiant spirits.
A ceremony. These films are festive.

Before the final credits, the hero puts his lips
into her hair, its utter blackness. That is all.

Richard Dove

Über die Bedeutung von Schlaf in Diyarbakir

Die Fiakerpferde am Tigris
haben papierne Nelken hinter dem Ohr.
Ihre Kutscher eingeschlafen über dem Trick-Track-
Spiel. Es kostet nur einen halben Tag.

In den Taxis sind die gelben Böden
mit Pistazienschalen bedeckt. Aber wer will
vorankommen? Im weißen Dampf der Sonne
brennst du ohne Feuer.

Auch der Löwe auf der seldschukischen Münze,
gerade auf dem Markt erstanden,
schläft, wenn du ihn silbern ins Licht hältst.
Eine Fliegenklatsche erledigt winzige Eidechsen.

Hier schlafen alle auf dem Dach ihrer Häuser.
Angenehm, daß der Schlaf keine albernen Fragen
stellt. Wozu bist du hier? Auf diesem unentschlossenen
Dach, und alle so ausgesucht freundlich?

Was du um fünf Uhr träumst, wird wahr.
Morgens um fünf ist die Zukunft schwarz.
Die Pferde erwachen, der Löwe gähnt silbrig,
das arme Hirn erschlägt den braunen Tigris.

from *Ich habe die Nacht*

On the meaning of sleep in Diyarbakir

The fiacre horses by the Tigris
sport paper carnations behind their ears.
Their coachmen have nodded off over their game of
trick-track. It only takes half a day.

In the taxis the yellow floors
are strewn with pistachio shells. But who wants
to make any headway? You burn without fire
in the sun's white vapour.

The lion too on this Seljuk coin
just bought at the market
is sleeping when you hold its silvery face to the light.
A fly-swat disposes of miniscule lizards.

Everyone sleeps on the roof of their house here.
It's pleasant that sleep doesn't ask any foolish
questions. Why are you here? On this irresolute roof
and everyone making such a point of being friendly?

What you dream at five will come true.
At five in the morning the future is black.
The horses wake up, the lion yawns its silvery yawn,
the wretched brain dispatches the brown Tigris.

Richard Dove

In der Art des Abu Nawas

Die Sommersterne finden ihre Lichtung
im Himmel. Sie leuchten auf die Weinkrüge
herab, ihren Turban aus feuchtem Lehm.

Der Wein weckt das Jagdherz. Er verspricht
Hügel und Wild. Trink, sagt er, koste, denn
vom erinnerten Leben bleibt nichts als die Frische

einzelner Sinne. Der Duft der aufgeschlagenen Mandel.
Das Klingeln der Silberkette an deinem Kinn.
Das Licht, grün und sanft, in den Gärten von Basra.

Trinken wir auf die vergangenen, die schönen Tage!
Auf den Dünenkamm weißer als weiß, weißer als
die Seite? Erinnerst du meine Worte auf der Seite?

Und den Papagei, röter als rot, neben dem Turban?
Röter als Blut? Erinnerst du das Blut? Erinnerst du
die Zikaden, die sich in uns zu langem Tode zirpten?

from *Ich habe die Nacht*

In the manner of Abu Nawas

The summer stars up there discover
a clearing. Down they shine
on pots of wine we stop with wet
turbans of clay that catch the glow.

Wine wakes the heart for hunting. Hills
and antelope it promises. Drink up, it says,
enjoy, for nothing of remembered life
is left but freshness of the single senses.

A shelled almond's aroma.
Your silver necklace, tinkling.
A green and soft light
in the gardens of Basra.

Shall we drink up then to good old times?
To the dune's ridge, whiter
than white, whiter still than paper –
do you recall these words of mine on it?

And to the parrot, redder than red, perching
beside a turban? Redder than blood?
Do you recall the blood? Recall, chirping
themselves to their long death in us, the cicadas?

Christopher Middleton

Elfenbein-Georgette

In Damaskus nannte man
den Schleier nach dem Stoff.
Er enthüllte den Schwung der Wangen
und was dem Hals folgte.
Im Himmel surrten die Drachen.

Im Innenhof lagerte das grüne,
von den Pflanzen verbliebene Licht.
Im blaßgrünen Licht lagerten wir.
Drehten uns, wendeten uns,
die schönsten Rundungen der Welt.

Belkis, die fette Lady, sang
vom Mund des Körpers, von Milch,
welche in diesen Mund sickerte.
Ihre Brüste hatten die Größe
von Boxhandschuhen. Wir lernten:

Schönheit ist nicht Wahrheit, und
Wahrheit kommt in verschiedenen Größen.
Ihr Lied ließ keine der schweren Fragen aus:
Nach was sehnen wir uns?
Zu wem gehören wir?

Wie lange kann Sehnen sich sehnen?
Ihre Hand hielt keine Kreide.
Ihr Lied wurde kalt wie Sirup.
Das Tuch über dem Vogelkäfig hatte
die Farbe von Elfenbein in Damaskus.

from *Ich habe die Nacht*

Ivory georgette

In Damascus they named
the veil after the fabric.
It enveloped the curve of a cheek
and what came after the throat.
In the sky a susurrus of kites.

Green from plants, the light
lay in the inner court.
In pale green light lay we,
we twisted and we turned
the world's most beautiful curves.

Belkis sang, the fat lady,
of the body's mouth, of milk
which trickled into it.
Her breasts were huge,
like boxing gloves. We learned a lesson:

Beauty is not truth, and truth
does come in different sizes.
Of questions that are hard her song
omitted none: What's longing for?
Whose property are we?

How long can longing last?
In her hand no chalk.
Her song went cold as sirup.
The cloth thrown over the birdcage
had an ivory hue in Damascus.

Christopher Middleton

In Tunis lügen die Palmen

Auf dem Klassenfoto sehen wir nicht so gut aus.
Alifa verhuscht, der Primus mit Unschuldsmiene,
Monique, für die ich schwärmte, schweigt
verschrammt. So vergilbt ist die Fotografie,
horizontaler Lichteinfall in Höhe der Köpfe
(wie die blonden Schaumfetzen am Strand),
daß der Betrachter meint, die Cephalogramme
der Schüler zu lesen. In ihrer Mitte, zierlich,
die Lehrerin. Jusqu'à l'os, sagte ich ihr,
bis zum Knochen. Sie wurde rot im weißen TGM,
rot wie – auf dem Boot vor der Insel Zembra –
die Kante von Monique. Weil keine Frau schöner ist
als das Verlangen nach einer Frau, flüstert
der arabische Freund. ,Wie sie durch ihre Beine
schaut. So groß ist sie!' und ritzt es ins Holz
der Schulbank. Monique (Vater: Araber, Mutter:
Französin) hatte den gleichen Heimweg wie ich,
vom weißen Bahnhof La Marsa nach Gammarth,
unter dem Gezischel uralter, rundlicher Palmen,
die noch heute stehen, die nicht die Wahrheit
sagen: Daß sich alles verändert hat, jedes, alles.

(Lycée de Carthage, Fotografie vom November 1958)

from *Ich habe die Nacht*

The palm-trees tell lies in Tunis

We don't look that swell on the class photograph.
Alifa, star pupil with his ingenuous mug, is blurred,
Monique, who I had a crush on, is wrapped in
scratchy silence. The photo's so yellowed –
at head-level a horizontal irruption of light
(like the blond scraps of foam on the beach) –
that the viewer imagines he's reading schoolchildren's
cephalograms. In their midst is the teacher,
slender. Jusqu'à l'os, I told her,
right down to the bone. She went red in the white TGM,
red as Monique's nook in the boat off
the island of Zembra. Because no woman's fairer
than the desire for a woman, my Arab friend
whispers. 'The way she's looking through her
legs. How tall she is!', and carves it into the wood
of the school-bench. Monique (father Arab, mother
French) walked home the same way as I did,
from the white station La Marsa to Gammarth,
beneath the furtive whispers of stocky, ancient palm-trees,
which still stand today, which don't tell the
truth: that everything's changed, each and everything.

(Lycée de Carthage, photograph from November 1958)

Richard Dove

Abdullah Frères, Constantinople

Weil er russische Offiziere, Feinde, in sein Haus geladen hatte,
zehn Zimmer, in denen es ein Klavier, Bronzefiguren,
                                        Spitzenvorhänge,
Schränke voller Bücher, Silber und Porzellan
und Dienstmädchen mit Federwisch gab,
entzog der Sultan Kevork Abdullah und seinen Brüdern,
Armeniern mit assimiliertem Namen, im Jahre 1878
das Recht, sich Fotografen seiner Majestät zu nennen.
Frühere Fotos von der *Sublime Porte* wurden konfisziert.

Doch der Handel blühte. Die Eitelkeiten blühten.
In Kairo gründeten die *Frères* eine Niederlassung.
In Paris informierten sie sich über die neuesten Techniken.
Die Paschas und ihre Kinder wollten scharfe *Cartes de cabinet*.
1890 wurden *Abdullah Frères* wieder Hoffotografen.
Sitz ihres Studios jetzt: 452 Grande Rue de Péra.

Doch Kevork, der ein Leben lang mit Gefallsucht zu tun hatte,
wurde bitter. 1900 verkaufte er
das Atelier an *Sébah & Joaillier*
für 12 000 osmanische Lira,
genug, um seine Schulden zu tilgen.
Er wollte, wie er ein Jahr später seiner armenischen Freundin in
                                                            Paris
schrieb, nur noch ‚auf die Stimme des Unendlichen hören',
die ihm manchmal aus duftenden Rosen zu kommen schien.
Er wußte, der Fotograf, daß jede Legende verblaßt,
und mit seinen Bildern das Gedächtnis
des letzten Sultans.

from *Ich habe die Nacht*

Abdullah Frères, Constantinople

He'd invited Russian officers, enemies, into his house—
ten rooms with a piano, bronzes, lace curtains,
cabinets full of books, silver, and porcelain,
and maids with feather dusters—so in 1878
the Sultan stripped Kevork Abdullah and his brothers,
Armenians with assimilated names, of the right
to call themselves His Majesty's photographers.
Earlier photos of the *Sublime Porte* were confiscated.

But business flourished. Vanities flourished.
The *Frères* opened a branch in Cairo.
In Paris, they learned the latest techniques. The pashas
and their children wanted sharp focus for *Cartes de cabinet*.
In 1890, *Abdullah Frères* became court photographers again.
The new address of their studio: 452 Grande Rue de Péra.

But Kevork, who had to deal all his life with vanity,
grew bitter. In 1900, he sold
the atelier to *Sébah & Joaillier*
for 12,000 Ottoman lira,
enough to pay off his debts.
As he wrote to his Armenian girlfriend in Paris one year later,
all he wanted now was to 'listen to the voice of the infinite'
he sometimes seemed to hear in fragrant roses.
The photographer knew that every legend fades,
and with its pictures the memory
of the last Sultan.

Andrew Shields

from *Mine is the night*

Salz am Hals

vor dem Ischtar-Tor im Pergamon-Museum, Berlin

Das Blau der Glasur stumpf. Der müde Ort. Der falsche Ort.
Müde, sagt Ischtar, weil man mich mit Liebe überzieht
wie mit Krieg. Müde, wegen dieses Kriegs schwarze Ränder
mir über das Auge zu malen. Sieh mein zweimal geteiltes Auge!
Du pflückst die weißen Linien aus ausgeblühtem Salz am Hals.
Müde der Unterschiede zwischen Morgen und Abend,
zwischen Land und Land. Müde des Körpers, des Lärms
der Hände unter der tiefen Haut. Die gelben Löwen sind
am Abend nur noch Spiegel. Am Morgen, wie das Museum
riecht! Ich habe mich in den Wärter verliebt, heimlich,
und zwei Wörter auf einmal gesagt: Liebe und Vergessen.

So lügt das Glas.
So klirren bläulich die Palmen.
So sind die Zeichen für den Tod der Königin.

from *Ich habe die Nacht*

Salt from my neck

in front of the Ishtar Gate in the Pergamon Museum, Berlin

Dull the blue of the glazing. This place is weary. Is wrong.
Weary, says Ishtar, because they're covering me with love
as though with war. Too weary because of this war to paint
black rims above my eye. Take a look at my eye, twice divided!
You're plucking the white lines of efflorescent salt from my neck.
Weary of the distinctions between morning and evening,
between orient, occident. Weary of the body, the blare
of hands beneath deep skin. The yellow lions are no more
than mirrors now in the evening. In the morning, oh the way
the museum smells! I've fallen in love with the attendant, secretly,
and uttered two words at once: love and oblivion.

That's how the glass lies.
That's how the palm-trees clink blueishly.
That's how the portents look which herald the death of the queen.

Richard Dove

Die erste Nacht

Die erste Nacht fing an.
Die Tür des Zimmers öffnete sich auf ein Zimmer.
Es war die Zeit, da die Boote sich in die Häuser zurückzogen.
Daß ein Segel in mir war, wunderte mich nicht.
Es klatschte. Es zählte meinen Puls.
Sein nasser Körper gefiel den Sinnen. Sie hielten
in diesem Zimmer mich gefangen. Ein Anfänger
lernte ich viel dazu:

Daß eine Frau sich in mir verteilen kann,
ohne sich um mich zu kümmern.
Daß ich jede Dämmerung, um schön zu werden,
in diesem Zimmer mich einzufinden habe.
Daß der Apfel der Hexe geteilt ist und hart.
Daß das Flickbuch, wenn du den Daumen richtig
anlegst, fünf Lagen hat: Der Vögel, Frauen und Läden,
der Selbstbildnisse, die sich unmerklich verändern,
der Schiffe mit bald vollem, bald schlaffem Segel.

Dann schließt sich der Hafen: Die erste Nacht.
Die See steigt an die Zunge.

from *Ich habe die Nacht*

The first night

The first night began.
The door of the room opened into a room.
It was the time when the boats drew back within the houses.
A sail in me seemed no cause for wonder.
It clapped. It counted my pulse.
Its wet body was gratifying to all the senses. I was kept
locked in this room. A beginner,
I have learned much:

That a woman can disperse herself within me
without caring for me;
that every twilight, in order to become beautiful,
I am compelled to this room;
that the apple of the witch is split in two and is hard;
that the flickered book, when you lay a thumb correctly to it,
has five layers: of birds, of women and shops,
of self-portraits, that change imperceptibly,
of ships with now filled and now loosened sails.

Then the harbour closes. The first night.
The sea rises to the tongue.

Robert Gray

Auf Salina

Niedrige Kaper bedeckt das Land.
Reiseführer, Liparische Inseln

Du sitzst an bröckeliger Brüstung,
Kopf im Spalier brüchiger Köpfe,
vor dir Landschaft, das karge Allerlei
des Meeres, sein Laut in Bogengängen
des Gehörs, fickfedernde Masten, Schütt-
Kies, Fliesen, Licht. Im Licht Wespen,
müde stichelnd wie dein alternder Bauch.

So segelst du im Hafen, zwischen Fähren,
die kommen und gehen, und verläßt
die Reede nicht. Der Wind hat gedreht,
die Wogen schicken Worte übers Laute
ins Licht, Laut und Licht in den Reim,
Schaum, und schau, rundes Auge,
in den schlaflosen Kopf auf dem Meer.

from *Ich habe die Nacht*

On Salina

Low caper bushes cover the country.
Travel guide, Liparian Islands

You crouch on the run-down ramparts,
head in the row of crumbling heads,
countryside before you, the sparse jumble
of the sea, its sound in the canals
of hearing, up-thrusting masts, bulk
gravel, tiles, light. In the light, wasps,
tiredly stabbing like your aging belly.

So you sail in the harbor, between ferries
coming and going, and do not leave
the roadstead. The wind has turned,
the waves send words over roaring
into light, sound and light into the rhyme,
spume, and spy, round eye,
into the sleepless head on the sea.

Andrew Shields

from *Mine is the night*   153

Bei Wiepersdorf, August

Vanitas-Sonnett

die Wiesen vor uns, ohne Wind,
sind grünstarrende erloschene Uhren
Kiefern riechen hier nach Harz
und sterben nach Bäumeart vom Kopf aus

brennen langsam ab wie Kerzen
das Blech des Autos kocht
aufgebahrt auf grauem Moos
neben polierten Nadeln und Wegen

wir gehen weiter unter andere
hohe und durstige Bäume
die Korridore der Erinnerung

berühren uns
das Glas für dich, aller Duft für mich
das knisternde Land, nieder stürzende Vögel

from *Ich habe die Nacht*

Near Wiepersdorf, August

vanitas sonnet

the meadows in front of us, windless,
are spent clocks staring greenly
pine-trees reek of resin here
and die the way trees do, from the head downwards

burning slowly down like candles
the car's metal body is boiling
lying in state on grey moss
alongside polished needles and paths

we walk on pass beneath other
lofty and thirsty trees
the corridors of memory

touch us
the glass for you, all fragrance for me
this crepitating land, crashing birds

Richard Dove

from *Mine is the night*

Freundschaft der Dichter

Wie Babel blättern wir
in den Wörterbüchern, gewaltig,
nicht wütend, freundlich mit denen,
die uns die Wörter brachten.
Sie stehen im Licht vor den Fenstern,
dahinter der Garten, die steinerne Bank,
darunter die Katze und die tote Maus,
daweiter die Reben, die Ordnung,
mit der wir Silben tauschen.

Kuppler sind wir. Wollen, daß
zwei fremde Zungen
sich heftig, ungezwungen
treffen. Der Wein hilft,
die Sonne, der große Raum
mit den Dichtern in so viel Licht
und raschelnden Büchern.

Das Mahl als Belohnung
am Abend. Ranken auf weißem Tuch.
Landesherrliche Speisen.
Zehn Finger legen wir auf sie.

from *Ich habe die Nacht*

Friendship between poets

We browse as Babel did,
mightily, through the lexicons,
not angry, friendly to those
who brought to us the words.
At windows they stand in the light,
the garden behind the stone bench,
the cat underneath it, the dead mouse,
and beyond to the vineyards, order
we trade our syllables for.

We're go-betweens. We want
two alien tongues to meet
under no compulsion
forcefully. The wine helps,
the sun, the big room containing
poets in so much light,
and rustling books.

Evenings, as our reward,
the meal, vine-shoots on the white cloth.
Princely dishes.
We pitch ten-fingered in.

Christopher Middleton

Erholung in Lagos

Dann komme ich eben im Juni,
nach der Regenzeit. Bis dahin versteck ich mich
hinter meiner Angelegenheit, den sieben
zerbrochenen Rippen. Da ist es dunkel,
aber warm und wenig. Wenig Notwendigkeiten,
will sagen. Nicht Wasser der Wüste.

Und muß ich das wirklich in Beziehung setzen?
Zu New York z.B. Kugelsichere Weste.
Nicht ganz die gleichen gelben cabs.
Wie ein schwarzer BH zu zwei (schwarzen)
eingerollten Kätzchen. Weniger feucht.
Weniger Videos ans Hirn geschnallt.

Die lassen nicht los, hier wie dort. Gut,
ich komme im Herbst. Furchtbar, wie Eis
am Stiel nach Holz schmeckt. Leben ist
Bilder sammeln, die Atem geben und
dir nehmen. Du flatterst, Hölzchen,
Seelchen, nervenfeucht, unter Palmen.

(Eko Hotel, 13.9.1999)

from *Ich habe die Nacht*

Recuperating in Lagos

Well then, I'll come in June,
when the rainy season's over. Till then I'll barricade myself
behind my business, these seven
broken ribs. It's dark there
but fresh and few. That is to say
few necessities. No desert water.

And must I really relate it to something?
E.g. to New York. A bullet-proof vest.
The yellow cabs, not quite the same.
Like a black bra to two (black)
curled-up kittens. Less moist.
Less videos strapped to your brain.

They keep pursuing you, here just like there. Okay,
I'll come in the autumn. Appalling
the way an ice-cream on its stick tastes of wood. Life means
collecting images which give breath and take it
away from you. You are fluttering, little match,
little soul, nerve-moist, beneath the palm-trees.

(Eko Hotel, 13.9.1999)

Richard Dove

Ice Memory

Eis fließt wie Wasser. In der Tiefe des Eises
sind die alten Klimate bewahrt, vielleicht
ein Schlüssel für die Apokalypse.

Von der Bibel kennen wir Sintflut und Plagen.
8000 Meter tief ist Schnee aus Platons Tagen.
Die Zeit der Maler von Lascaux bei 17 000.

Im Eis von Grönland ist vulkanische Asche
von Krakatau, Bleiverschmutzung von alten
römischen Hochöfen und aus der Mongolei

herüber geblasener Staub. Es gibt Bläschen
in jeder Schicht, die von vergangenen Atmosphären
berichten, den abrupten, karnevalesken

Umschwüngen, erhalten über Tausende von Jahren.
Überhaupt verheißt der ungeheure Abstand eine Folge
von Ewigkeiten. Aus der Nähe ist es, als wolle

ein verrückter Bungee-Springer auf einer klapprigen
Achterbahn in rasendem Abflug landen. Doch
uns bewegt ohnehin nur eine Frage:

Wo ist der Abdruck unserer winzigen, nackten Füße?
Es gibt ein strafendes Muster von schöner Regelmäßigkeit:
Der Sommerschnee wird vom Winterschnee begraben.

Manche Eisberge haben einen erstaunlich blauen Glanz.
Das hat mit der Dichte des Eises zu tun, von zierlichen
Füßen dicht getreten, erklären die Spezialisten der Gletscher.

from *Ich habe die Nacht*

Ice memory

Ice flows like water. In the depths of the ice
the old climates are preserved, maybe
a key to the Apocalypse.

From the Bible we know floods and plagues.
The snow from the days of Plato is eight thousand metres deep,
from the time of the painters of Lascaux, seventeen thousand.

In the ice of Greenland there is volcanic ash
from Krakatoa, lead pollution from ancient
Roman blast furnaces, and from Mongolia

blown-in dust. In every layer there are tiny bubbles
telling us about past atmospheres,
the abrupt, carnival-like

changes, maintained for thousands of years.
Such distances promise a chain
of eternities. Close-up, it's as though

a crazy bungee-jumper wanted to land on a flimsy
rollercoaster at its speedy take-off. But
only one question moves us really:

where is the imprint of our tiny, naked feet?
There is a punitive pattern, a beautiful regularity:
the summer snow gets buried by the winter snow.

Some icebergs have an astonishing blue glimmer.
It is the density of the ice, from the dainty feet
treading there, says the expert in glaciers.

Robert Gray

Lilia Brik mit Majakovskij in Samarkand

Undatierte Fotografie

Die Schatten sind gesprächig, obwohl sie nicht sprechen werden.
Das Licht spricht auf seine Weise: Ein stummer Lichtwinkel
quer über dem Boden, wie ein schlafender Körper. Und
Majakovskij spricht nicht, und Lilia lächelt. Weil sie nicht
sprechen können (es ist ja eine Fotografie) scheint uns,
sie tragen viele, zu viele Geheimnisse in sich herum.

Rast in Samarkand bei einer Imbißbude. Zwei Männer stehen
hinter der Auslage (Zwei Töpfe. Teigwaren? Früchte?),
ein dritter hinter flach auf der Erde gestapelten Kisten.
Im Vordergrund Lilia auf einer Holzbank, Majakovskij
auf usbekischem Rohrstuhl. Beide mit Wanderstöcken.
Alle fünf schauen in die Kamera. Wer nimmt auf? Ossip?

Sie lächelt nicht Ossip an. Es ist Sommer. Ihre Schultern sind
rund, braun. Sie ist entschlossen, die unwiederholbare Liebe
im Leben eines großen Dichters zu sein. Das sieht man.
Tatiana, die Rivalin in Paris, wird diesen Vicomte heiraten.
Noch ein paar Jahre, und Majakovskij schießt sich eine Kugel
durch den Kopf in der Lubianskij-Gasse. Er sieht schon jetzt

nicht glücklich aus. Aber die entspannte Pose – aus schwarzem
Unterhemd mit weißer Bordüre ausgestreckter Arm, Feldherren-
hand auf Knauf – übertüncht alles. ‚Ich mag es nicht ohne dich‘,
hatte er dieser Tatiana per Telegramm mitgeteilt. Jetzt ist er hier.
Er hat dicke Melonenkerne ausgespuckt. Die grüne Moschee ist,
so die Verfügung der Soviets, Quartier für den Arbeiterverein.

Sonst ist alles einladend, großzügig fast. Am oberen Rand
der Fotografie die Ränder der Oase. Es ist heiß. Erst der Abend
wird diese Ordnung verwirren, mit Vögeln, mit Kamelen
aus Buchara, Luftschiffen aus dem Hinterland. Vier Männer,
eine Frau. Eine Frau und ein Mann. Im Kopf des Mannes
ein Bienenkorb von Frauen. Er ist so gesucht, so höflich (angeblich)

from *Ich habe die Nacht*

Lilia Brik with Majakovsky in Samarkand

Undated photograph

The shadows are talkative, although they say nothing.
The light speaks in its way: a mute angle of light
diagonally on the floor, like a sleeping body. And
Majakovsky does not speak, and Lilia smiles. Because they cannot
speak (it is, of course, a photograph), there is the feeling
that they carry many, too many, secrets within them.

Resting in Samarkand at a kiosk. Two men stand
behind the display (pots, pastries, fruits?),
a third is behind low boxes laid flat on the earth.
In the foreground Lilia has the wooden bench, Majakovsky
is on a wicker chair of Usbekistan. Both with walking sticks.
All five look at the camera. Who takes this? Ossip,

her husband? She does not smile. It is summer. Her shoulders are
round and brown. She is determined to be the unrepeatable love
in the life of a great poet. One can see that.
Tatiana, the rival in Paris, will have to marry her Vicomte.
And in a few years Majakovsky shoots a bullet
through his head, in Lubiansky Street. Now already he looks

uneasy. But his pose – contrived of black
undershirt with white edging, outstretched arm, commander's
hand on the knob – puts a whitewash on everything. 'I do not
                                    like it without you',
he has informed Tatiana by telegram. But he is here.
He has spat fat melon seeds at his feet. The green mosque,
by order of the Soviets, is a camp for the worker's society.

Apart from this, everything is inviting, generous almost. At the
                                    topmost edge
of the photograph, the borders of the oasis. It is hot. Though evening
will confuse this order, with birds, with camels
from Buchara, airships from the hinterland. Four men,
one woman. One woman and one man. In the man's head
a beehive of women. He is much sought after, and so polite
                                    (reputedly),

und wird heute nacht auf dem Registan vor 5000 lesen.
Doch in die gewaltsame Veränderung der Gesellschaft ist er
nicht so vernarrt wie früher. Seine Themen, immer öfter, stur:
Unerwiderte Liebe, Einsamkeit, Zerstörung. ,Ich bin so einsam
wie das einzige Auge eines Mannes auf dem Weg zu den Blinden.'
Die Sprünge in den Gefäßen repariert man hier mit Gold.

Nie ist uns ein so scharfes Bild begegnet. Wegen der Verkürzung
kann man nicht in die Holzkisten sehen. Besser so. Die Vögel
regen sich. Lilia: ein leichtes Schwindelgefühl. Ossip: abwesend.
Majakovskij: Durst in einer Wüstenei von Überzeugungen.
Heute abend, lesend, wird er sich an Seide und Sinn beruhigen.
Wann kommt die Nacht, und mit der Nacht endlich

der ornithologische Zauber? Flügel, Schwärme, Schnörkel,
die nicht zur Wahrheit gehören. Ein Schwindelgefühl.
Wußte er viel von Frauen? Auf der Fotografie immer
noch Mittag, steiles Licht. Kein Zwielicht. Gezielter Blick
nur. Die Kartuschen der Liebe. Blendende Schachzüge aus Eis.
Man muß dies alles ersinnen aus verblichenen Erinnerungen

und *zum Augenblick eindicken* mit dem Weiß des Kleides,
dem Schwarz des Unterhemds, dem vergilbten Müll
am Rand der Sträucher, dem Weiß ihrer Augen, man muß
den Streit ersinnen und die endlosen, sinnlosen Wechsel
von Briefen, Telegrammen, Telefonaten, zu ersinnenden
Gefechten der Liebe und der überbelichteten Müdigkeit.

from *Ich habe die Nacht*

and will read this evening at the Registan in front of five thousand.
But a forcible change in society
does not obsess him as before. His themes are more frequently
                                                      stubborn:
unrequited love, loneliness, destruction. 'I am so lonely,
like the single eye of a man on the pathways to the blind.'
Here one repairs the cracks in the vessel with gold.

Never before have we had so clear a picture. Because of its
                                                      reduction
we cannot see into the boxes. It is better like that. The birds
stir. Lilia: light-headedness. Ossip: absent.
Majakovsky: a chaos among convictions.
This evening, as he reads, he will calm himself with silk and with
                                                      meanings.
When does the night come, and with the night

an ornithological magic? Wings, swarms, ornamental scrolls
that don't belong to reality. A feeling of dizziness.
Did he know much of women? In the photograph it's
still midday, a steep light. Nothing twilit. Directed glances
only. The cartridges of love. Blinding chess-moves of ice.
One must invent all this from a bleached memory

and *within a moment thicken it*, with the whiteness of the dress,
the black of the undershirt, the yellowed rubbish
on the edge of the bushes, the whites of their eyes; one must
invent the arguments and the endless, senseless exchange
of letters, telegrams, phone calls, and also the impending
dangers of love, and of an overexposed weariness.

                                                      Robert Gray

Antlitz

für Marwan

Die Stille reift
wie Steine eine Rinde bilden
der Stoff darunter von der gleichen Materie
wie die Oberfläche
bis zum Grund ändert sich nichts
umsonst hackt der Blick auf Raum auf Zeit
überall ist das Gesicht offen da

Die Löcher in dem Gesicht
sind Brunnen aus denen die Stille
steigt Erinnerungen aus Silben und Vornamen

So ist der Kopf aus Schrift
Auch die Schrift bildet eine Haut
das Fleisch darunter auch aus Schrift
Manchmal fließt ein Gesicht in ein anderes
Pinselstriche sind Kürzel für das Leben
Sie bannen den Tod weil sie ihn üben

Dieses Gesicht ist eine Welt
denn es gibt nur das Gesicht
gebaut und verworfen und
wieder errichtet vibrierend
vom Tod in das Leben und
zurück plötzlich Antlitz
unauslöschbar

Kein Unterschied mehr
zwischen Spiegel und Glas
und zurückgegebenem Blick
mein Blick
will dieses Antlitz sein

from *Ich habe die Nacht*

Countenance

for Marwan

The silence ripens
as stones form a crust
the stuff beneath it of the same material
as the surface
all the way down nothing changes
in vain the gaze hacks at space at time
everywhere the face is open there

The holes in the face
are springs the silence emerges from
memories made of syllables and first names

Thus is the head made of writing
Even the writing forms a skin
the flesh beneath is also writing
Sometimes a face flows into another
brushstrokes are shorthand for life
They banish death by practising it

This face is a world
for there is only the face
built and condemned and
erected again vibrating
from death into life and
back suddenly countenance
indelible

No more difference
between mirror and glass
and the gaze given back
my gaze wants
to be this countenance

Andrew Shields

Alterskunde

Nur einige wenige Stellen, die so sind
wie vor dreißig Jahren. Nicht das Gesicht.
Der Übergang vom Schlüsselbein zur Schulter,
vom Schenkel in das Knie. Sonst nichts.

Zwischen mir ist ein Flattern. Als habe
ein Schmetterling das Loch verlassen und
ein anderer es betreten. Als sie sagte:
‚Liebst du mich?' nahm ich mein Hemd

und log. Wenn ich jetzt fortgehe,
war ich nie fort gewesen. Ich glaubte,
es wäre Liebe. Wie könnte ich mir
eine Liebe vorstellen, unbeschienen,

von Nirgends nach Nirgends fließend,
und tief in der Erde begraben, wie
ein unterirdischer Strom? Das Gesicht.
Die Scham. Weggesteckt in eine Bucht

aus verschwiegenen Schatten, die von
den umliegenden Hügeln gebildet wird.
Ein langes wulstiges Lächeln, in dem der Nabel
versteckt sein muß. Die Stellen. Der Druck.

Gerontological

Only a few places that are as they were
thirty years ago. Not the face.
The transition from collarbone to shoulder,
from thigh to knee. Nothing else.

Between me there's a flutter. As though
a butterfly had left the hole and
another had entered it. When she said,
'Do you love me?' I picked up my shirt

and lied. If now I were to go away,
never I've been away. I thought
it was love. How could I
imagine a love not irradiated,

flowing from Nowhere to Nowhere,
and buried deep in the earth, like
a subterranean river? The face.
The pudenda. Put away into

a bay of shadows not talked about,
formed by the hills that surround them.
A long pouting smile in which the navel
must be concealed. The marks. The urge.

Michael Hamburger

Weg ins Ende

Abgestuckte Fassaden, durchgetretene Entrées:
Berlin-Charlottenburg mit seinen Jahrhundert –
Posen am Ende: mit Pressform und High Touch
werden die Kriegskinder auf neue Zeiten getrimmt.

Werden tragen, was hebt, türkt, stretcht, stützt.
Doppelmoral als Wonderbra – Krayatiden.
Das Alter: nur Träume des Körpers noch.
Der Rest des Wegs: Stimmungen in Geiselhaft

unter hochverschrammter Kapuzen-Nacht.
Trommelnd buchstabiert sie das Schicksal,
hustet, macht die Kehle vom Marmorkuchen
frei: für jenen Durst, zu brechen, zu täuschen,

es einmal noch zu machen, ein Möglich
an die Millionen Möglich zu fügen. Im Museum
zeigt eine Rampe von 100 Metern die dreizehn
Milliarden-Jahre-Geschichte des Universums.

Die Ära der Dinosaurier nimmt die letzten
drei schuppigen Meter ein, das Zeitalter
der Menschen hat die Breite eines Haars.
Wir schauen hinauf in prasselnde Sterne.

Zeiss heißt die Stimme des Kosmos. Wo all
das steht? In deinem Kopf. Ein Wind
aus Brandenburg schiebt den Schwefel fort.
Ein Wind, totenstill. Stiftet, was bleibt.

from *Ich habe die Nacht*

Path to the end

Façades stuccoless and footsore hallways:
Berlin-Charlottenburg's run through its
centennial poses: with moulds and High Touch
the children of war are being licked into shape for a new age.

They'll wear what lifts, fakes, stretches, supports.
Double standards qua wonderbra – crayatids.
Old age: no more now than dreams of the body.
The rest of our path: a hostage's humours

beneath a heavily-scuffed hooded night.
Drumming, this night spells out destiny,
coughs and liberates the throat of marble cake:
clearing the way for that thirst to break, dupe,

start over again, add one's own maybe
to the myriads of maybes. In the museum
a ramp 100 metres long shows
the history of the universe, thirteen billion years.

The dinosaur era takes up the last
three scaly metres, the epoch
of man is as broad as a hair.
We squint up into pelting stars.

Zeiss is the voice of the cosmos. Where is
all this stored? In your head. A wind
from Brandenburg elbows the sulphur away.
A wind, still as death. Creates what will remain.

Richard Dove

from *Mine is the night*   171

Die Schatten unter den Wellen

für Emilio Vedova

I Aus dem Augenrund

Ein falscher Schritt der Sonne
und schon stockt die Sprache,
Wirbel, Löcher in ihrem Fluß.

Kreiselnd fluten die Worte zurück
in die Reuse der Augen.
Der Liebe doppelte Pforte:

Aug und Augenschlitz.
Daß sie weit aufstehen
in den Haaren

für der Milch, der Schatten Schwall.
Für einen neuen Versuch:
Aus dem Augenrund zu brechen

wie der Maler aus seinem Bildgeviert.
Seine Zunge will die Gliederung
der Welt verstehen, ihren Atem,

der herrlich verwildert.
Nicht nur die Zunge,
auch die Hand, der Pinsel.

Der unsteten Augen flüssiger Pinsel.

II

Das Bild ist kein Spiegel.
Malen ist einem unbekannten Gesicht
die Augen bieten.

Seit Jahren gräbst du
dein um- und umgemaltes Grab.

from *Ich habe die Nacht*

The shadows under the waves

for Emilio Vedova

I From the orb of the eye

The sun takes one false step
and already language falters,
whirlpools, holes in its flow.

Circling, the words flood back
into the hoop net of the eyes.
The doubled door of love:

eye and slit of the eye.
That they are wide open
in the hairs

for milk's, for shadow's flow.
For one more attempt:
to escape from the orb of the eye

like the painter from the square of his picture.
His tongue wants to understand the arrangement
of the world, its breath,

gone gloriously wild.
Not just the tongue,
but the hand, the brush.

The restive eyes' fluent brush.

II

The picture is not a mirror.
Painting is baring your eyes
to an unknown face.

For years you've been digging
your painted and repainted grave.

III

Molto inquieto della morte
Lorenzo Lotto

Die Farbe riecht nach Gedächtnis.
Schrunden, Windtrichter, Risse
laufen in ihr herum.

Sie ist Membran
zwischen Festem und Fließendem,
von Licht durchpflügt und von Schatten.

Sie pocht mit dem Auge des Malers,
ohne Uhrwerk zu sein, sein Gegenteil
eher, Zeit überspringend,

ein freieres Spiel, von unserer Zeit
und zeitlos. Dieses Spiel
lehrt uns:

Was Licht und Raum ist,
was Tumult, was vielleicht Seele,
die zu lesen kaum uns bleibt.

IV

Venedig: Eine Welt, gebaut von
Markt- und Wassergeräuschen,
Farben, als erhebe sich die Lagune
zu einem Lebenszeichen aus Schiff und Stern.

Reflexe, Netze des Wassers,
als nähere sich eine Armada,
in großen Werften frisch gezimmert.

‚Die höchste Spannung', von der Gigi sprach,
ist hier: ‚Eine Welle aus Kraft
und Licht', die durchlittene Welle.

Die Schatten unter dieser Welle
geben, am Dorsoduro, Ahnung
vom Meer, wie es kracht und singt

from *Ich habe die Nacht*

III

Molto inquieto della morte
Lorenzo Lotto

The paint smells of memory.
Cracks, wind craters, fractures
run around in it.

It is a membrane
between the fixed and the flowing,
plowed through by light and by shadow.

It ticks with the eye of the painter,
without being a clockwork, its opposite
rather, skipping over time,

a freer game, of our time
and timeless. This game
teaches us:

what light and space are,
and tumult, and perhaps soul,
which is hardly left for us to read.

IV

Venice: a world, made of
market and water sounds,
colors, as if the lagoon were rising
towards a sign of life from ship and star.

Reflexes, nets of water,
as if an armada were approaching,
newly made in great shipyards.

'The greatest tension,' of which Gigi spoke,
is here: 'A wave of power
and light,' the wave endured.

The shadows under this wave
give, on the Dorsoduro, a sense
of the sea, how it crashes and sings

weiter draußen. Hereingeholt, heiter
auf einmal, zwischen Brücken und so vielen
freudigen Linien für den Blick.

V

Philipp Otto Runge sagte, es gebe
durchsichtige und undurchsichtige,
‚körperliche' Farben. Ein gutes Beispiel
sei das undurchsichtige Weiß, oder Schwarz.
Dem widerspricht der Maler:
Daß aus mehr und mehr Schatten
kein Licht entstehen kann. ‚Dann soll
das Sterngefild mit grauer Flamme brennen!
Beflimmert, beleuchtet von meiner Unruhe!'

Und er sagt auch:
‚Wenn selbst das Wort „schwarz"
schwarz klingen kann, so kann
schwarz ausschauen das gemalte All.'
So kann die Reinheit des Blicks
aufstellen eine Grammatik des Lichts.

further out. Brought in, blithe
suddenly, between bridges and so many
gleeful lines for the gaze.

V

Philipp Otto Runge said there are
transparent and non-transparent,
'corporeal' colors. A good example
is non-transparent white, or black.
The painter contradicts that
from more and more shadows
can come no light. 'Then let
the fields of stars burn with a gray flame!
Shimmered, illuminated by my restlessness!'

And he also says:
'If even the word "black"
can sound black, black can
be the look of the painted universe.'
Thus can the purity of the gaze
establish a grammar of light.

Andrew Shields

from *Mine is the night*

Im Paradies

Es gab Schlangen und Grasschlangen.
Es gab Schwänze und Fischschwänze.
Es gab Sonne und Mond und es gab
Sonnenmond. Überhaupt gab es alles.
Auch die Sterblichkeit und ihr Lied.

Es gab jede Menge Bilder, Archive,
Museen. Die Jäger waren unterwegs.
Einige spezialisierten sich auf die Vulva,
wie sie das Leben eröffnet. Andere
auf die Unendlichkeit der Musik. Sie

verloren sich glücklich darin. Wieder
andere erkannten sich in den festgelegten
Räumen der Malerei. Wir schrieben.
Die Fangeisen der Zeit blitzten herrlich.
Es gab Angst und Anmut und Aufstand.

Es gab Passhöhen und Adler.
Passhöhen mit Panzern gibt es.
Gnadenwasser für die Blumen gibt es.
Geborstene Pupillen, Schaft ohne Glieder
gibt es. Gewalt gibt es. Wohltuende

Nacht gibt es. Unkaputtbare Menschen
gibt es nicht. Vergebung von Rache
gibt es nicht. Vertrauen gibt es nicht.
Zukunft gibt es nicht. Das Paradies treibt
Schreie aus der Brust, Fliegen zur Wunde.

from *Ich habe die Nacht*

In paradise

Snakes there were and grass-snakes.
Tails there were and fish-tails.
There was sun and moon and there was
sunmoon. In actual fact, there was everything.
Mortality too and its song.

There were any number of pictures, archives,
museums. The hunters were out on the prowl.
Some became specialists of the vulva,
the way it opens existence. Others
of the infinity of music – they

blissfully lost themselves in it. Others still
recognised themselves in painting's
delimited realms. We got on with writing.
Time's snares were sparkling splendidly.
There was dread and grace and insurrection.

Mountain passes there were and eagles.
Mountain passes with tanks there are.
Mercy water for flowers there is.
Exploded pupils, trunks without limbs
there are. There is violence. There's

soothing night. Unbreakable people
there are not. Forgiveness of vengeance
there is not. There is no trust.
There is no future. Paradise drives
screams out of chests, flies into wounds.

Richard Dove

Notes and Afterword

Notes

Embrace of the birds (p. 7) The first stanza is partly influenced by Freud's essay on Leonardo.

Love and work (p. 13) 'snowbreak damage' occurs in winter, to conifers in particular, when boughs break due to an excessive burden of snow, hoar-frost or ice.

The Cyprus silence (pp. 15ff) The quotations in the first poem are from letters Rimbaud sent to his family in Charleville while he was working in Cyprus, whereas those in the second poem are purely imaginary, although a little in line with the correspondence between Rimbaud and his beloved sister Vitalie.

Light blue, with moon (p. 33) Orhan Veli Kanik (1914-50) was Turkey's first modern poet and, together with Nazim Hikmet, its most popular, liberating the poem from all traditions and emphasising spontaneity and daily speech. Tezer Kiral, an Istanbul writer, died very young of cancer in 1985; her four small books (*The cold nights of childhood, On tracing Cesare Pavese* et al.) are bold in style, broke many taboos and brought her almost mythical fame among the *literati* of Istanbul. Both writers, who had not known each other, are buried close to each other in a beautiful old cemetery above the Bosporus near the Rumeli Hisar fortress.

To a dolphin in Batumi (p. 41) Batumi is a port on the west coast of the Black Sea. It goes back to the Greek settlement Bathys, not far from Tomis, the place to which Ovid was banished.

Believing in make-believe tales (p. 47) An elegy for Paul Celan, who drowned in the Seine in 1970.

Abdo Rimbo (p. 57) 'Abdo Rimbo' is the legend on the seal which Arthur Rimbaud used in Harar, Ethiopia.

Graves (p. 79) Gottfried Benn (1886-1956) was the most controversial German poet of the twentieth century (because of his short flirtation with Nazi doctrine) and, after Rilke, the most influential. A doctor for venereal diseases, he practised in his later years (and died) in an apartment in the Steglitz district of Berlin (Bozener Straße 20). There is a commemoration plate at the entrance to the house.

A photograph of J.P. (p. 81) The initials are those of the Hungarian poet János Pilinszky (1921–81). His collection *Requiem*, which contains the 'Ravensbrück Passion', appeared in Budapest in 1964.

Alexandria: A cycle (pp. 85ff) This cycle revolves around the figure of Constantine Cavafy and his home. The first poems were written shortly after a journey from Cyprus, where I was living, to Alexandria in 1986 to explore the poet's haunts. The 'Three unpublished poems from the estate of Constantine Cavafy' are fictitious. My research was aided above all by E.M. Forster's *Alexandria: A History and A Guide* (1922, 1982), Marguerite Yourcenar's long essay *Poèmes de Constantin Cavafy* (1958) and Robert Liddell's *Cavafy: A Biography* (1976). The cycle – originally just four poems long - was first published in 1992 but has been added to in subsequent collections.

Alexandria (3) (p. 109) In his day, Professor Breccia was one of the main authorities on the Greco-Roman remains in Alexandria.

Ayios Kassianos (p. 135) The name of a Greek quarter in the old part of the divided capital of Cyprus, Nicosia (Lefkosia), directly abutting the boundary with the Turkish zone. Lapta: a town in the hills of northern Cyprus. 'Pakistani bush': the way the Cypriots style the shrub in question.

In the manner of Abu Nawas (p. 141) Abu Nawas, who was born in 757 and died in Baghdad in 815, is regarded as one of the greatest Arab poets and as one of the first *libertins* in world literature. In the service of the caliph of Baghdad, he was compelled to praise his patron but was at the same time devoted to wine, taverns and young boys, and had to go into exile several times due to unruly behaviour.

The palm-trees tell lies in Tunis (p. 145) The title of the German original ('In Tunis lügen die Palmen') is that of a drawing by Sigmar Polke. 'TGM' is an abbreviation for Tunis-Goulette-Marsa, the main stations served by a pre-colonial white-painted train, which still runs, connecting Tunis with the beaches on the Gulf of Tunis and passing through Carthage, Hamilcar and Sidi-Bou-Said. 'Jusqu'à l'os' is a very vulgar French expression, meaning to penetrate a woman very deeply.

In a lexicon of Berlin writers, it says:

> Joachim Sartorius, born in 1946 in Carthage. I liked that; in fact, I only came to Tunis at the age of ten, went to the Lycée de Carthage, and – during my first winter there - discovered silver Punic coins after heavy rainfall in the puddles in the schoolyard. That moulded me, along with the light in Sidi-Bou-Said, the dancer Aziza, the ruins of the Roman cities of Dougga and Sbeitla, the atomised splendour of the souks, the evanescence and the plenitude. There, on the African coast of

the Mediterranean, I turned very early into a sceptical hedonist who knew intuitively that 'there is a lot on offer'. It disintegrates quickly. That's probably the reason why I've so often shifted from contemplation to vita activa and back again.

(from an address to the German Academy for
Language and Literature, Darmstadt, 2003)

Near Wiepersdorf, August (p. 155) Wiepersdorf is the name of a small village forty miles from Berlin, lost in the flat and sandy pine-tree forests of Brandenburg, but well known for its mansion, which was the home of the Romantic poet Achim von Arnim (who died there in 1831) and of his wife Bettina von Arnim, the sister of the poet Clemens von Brentano. The mansion with its beautiful park was a residence for writers in GDR times.

Path to the end (p. 171) 'wonder*bra* – *cray*atids' is a play on words rather than a printing error. 'Creates what will remain': the original has an additional irony which refuses to travel into English - 'Stiftet, was bleibt' is an echo of a much-quoted line by Hölderlin ('Was aber bleibet, stiften die Dichter' – 'What remains though the poets create'). 'Zeiss' is the name of a famous optical firm, founded in 1846 in Jena by the industrialist Carl Zeiss; in Germany, Zeiss is still a synonym for precision, top-class mechanical performance and a means of exploring the universe.

The shadows under the waves (pp. 173ff) 'Gigi' is the name the Venetian-born Italian composer Luigi Nono was affectionately given by his friends, especially Emilio Vedova and Massimo Cacciari.

In paradise (p. 179) The poem varies a structural principle underlying Inger Christensen's long poem 'alphabet' (there are,… there are), and is also intended as a homage to this great Danish poet.

MAN FEARS TIME.
TIME FEARS THE PYRAMID.

Cheops

Instead of a Postscript

Five Observations

Christopher Middleton

1. 'On the way to the tomb of Kleoboulos'. K. (Latinised as Cleobulus) was one of the Seven Sages of Antiquity. A supposed tomb is situated in the vicinity of Lindos, on the east coast of Rhodes. The acutely personal poem addresses language itself as a source of healing virtues; the 'stone' would be petrifaction of accumulated dust; 'dust' the debris of stone crushed under Fortune's wheel; 'language' – the *driver*? Or Krishna? [*Sprache*, feminine gender in IE languages.]

2. Conrad on the Mediterranean: 'that old sea of magicians, slave-dealers, exiles, and warriors, the sea of legends and terrors, where the mariners of remote antiquity used to hear the restless shade of an old wanderer weep aloud in the dark' (*The Mirror of the Sea*, pp. 297–8).

3. J.S., brought up in Tunis, and though travelled in most parts of the globe, focuses in many poems on Mediterranean scenes, past and present: the habitat of his imagination (Muse). – A further variation on the motifs in the Hellenism of Germans since at least Winckelmann (1750s) [Lessing, Heinse, Goethe, Schiller, Hölderlin, Platen]. But neither on the lines of an aesthetic Idealism, nor on the lines of a demonism (as in Eichendorff's *The Marble Statue* (1819) and Thomas Mann's *Death in Venice*). J.S. is more inclined to celebrate, quietly, in his *murmuring voice*, certain remnants, not least for the phosphorescence he detects in and around them, those of the Ottoman-Levantine 'decadence', – the erotic.

4. Murmuring voice – the Levant [N.B. 'Levant' means *rising*, as of the sun in the east, which in Greek would be ανατολή, hence Anatolia too]. Certainly the mode is most usually elegiac, but it is not ever declamatory or high-minded. There are poems apropos the Alexandrian Cavafy, but the quiet, insistent, and exploratory

voice, unraised, is also consistent with Cavafy's. [Contrast: John Donne's Orient; a *figure* of *Resurrection*.]

5. 'Clash of civilisations': the 'endgame' of the Occident, e.g. Samuel Beckett, versus the revenge-game of the extreme Islamists – but little echo of Armageddon in J.S.'s poems... Still, they are attuned and sympathetic to those traditions in poetry which are an *ethereal* dimension of the 'true' Islam (poetry ranging from the most fragile and secret personal touches to the metaphysical and panoramic and muscular chants for desert divinities). To that extent, this murmuring voice, utterly devoid of anything theatrical or 'strutting', prolongs the 'endgame', offers an issue from its obsessional *retrospectiveness*, does it? The burden of the past, its *poetic* ingredient, merely a fume? Or might the murmur be a *sign* that, if only the militancy were stopped, a conciliation in the deep might be achieved? [Nothing doctrinally Xtian in J.S.]

Austin, Texas, February 2005